Quilling
for Scrapbooks
& Cards

Quilling
for Scrapbooks
& Cards

Susan Lowman

Sterling Publishing Co., Inc. New York
A Sterling/Chapelle Book

Chapelle, Ltd., Inc., P.O. Box 9252, Ogden, UT 84409

(801) 621-2777 • (801) 621-2788 Fax
e-mail: chapelle@chapelleltd.com
Web site: www.chapelleltd.com

Every effort has been made to ensure that all information in this book is accurate. However, due to differing conditions, tools, and individual skills, the publisher cannot be responsible for any injuries, losses, and/or other damages which may result from the use of the information in this book.

Due to limited amount of available space, we must print our patterns at a reduced size in order to give our patrons the maximum number of patterns possible in our publications. We believe the quality and quantity of our patterns will compensate for any inconvenience this may cause.

This volume is meant to stimulate craft ideas. If readers are unfamiliar or not proficient in a skill necessary to attempt a project, we urge that they refer to an instructional book specifically addressing the required technique.

Library of Congress Cataloging-in-Publication Data available

Lowman, Susan.
  Quilling for scrapbooks & cards / Susan Lowman.
      p. cm.
  Includes index.
  ISBN 1-4027-1922-1
  1. Paper quillwork. I. Title.

TT870.L733 2005
745.54--dc22

2005012909

10 9 8 7 6 5 4 3
Published by Sterling Publishing Co., Inc.
387 Park Avenue South, New York, NY 10016
©2005 by Susan Lowman
Distributed in Canada by Sterling Publishing
c/o Canadian Manda Group, 165 Dufferin Street
Toronto, Ontario, Canada M6K 3H6
Distributed in Great Britain by Chrysalis Books Group PLC,
The Chrysalis Building,
Bramley Road, London W10 6SP, England
Distributed in Australia by Capricorn Link (Australia) Pty. Ltd.
P. O. Box 704, Windsor, NSW 2756, Australia
Printed and Bound in China
All Rights Reserved

Sterling ISBN 1-4027-1922-1

For information about custom editions, special sales, premium and corporate purchases, please contact Sterling Special Sales Department at (800)805-5489 or specialsales@sterlingpub.com.

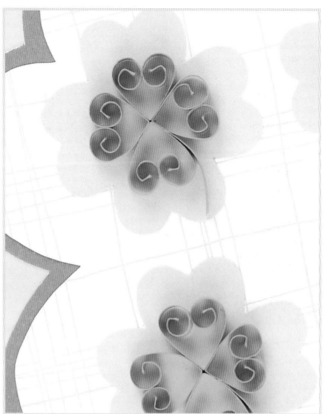

Table of Contents

Introduction to Paper Quilling

Welcome to the art of "paper quilling," also known as "paper filigree," or simply "quilling." Paper quilling is an old art form, that dates back over 500 years to the Renaissance, when nuns used elaborate quilling to decorate reliquaries (small boxes, caskets, or shrines in which relics are kept and shown). Since then, quilling has been used to decorate furniture, sconces, tea caddies, boxes, framed art, and much more. Today, quilling is more contemporary, making its way onto cards and scrapbook pages in new and exciting shapes.

Quilling is nothing more than rolling, shaping, and arranging strips of paper to make beautiful designs. It is easy and fun to do. The supplies are basic and inexpensive: quilling tools, strips of paper, a ruler, and adhesive. With these four basic supplies and some paper-crafting materials, you will be able to create many of the beautiful quilled cards and scrapbook pages in this book.

I hope you enjoy making these cards and scrapbook pages as much as I enjoyed designing them.

The Basics

Supplies

Quilling Tools and Supplies

There are a few supplies necessary for paper quilling, some of which you may already have.

Adhesive: High-quality, clear-drying craft glue should be used for quilling. White school glue is too thin, and does not set quickly enough to timely proceed to the next shape.

Quilling papers: Precut strips of 17"–24" quilling papers come in six widths: narrow ($\frac{1}{16}$"), standard ($\frac{1}{8}$"), quarter ($\frac{1}{4}$"), wide ($\frac{3}{8}$"), $\frac{1}{2}$", and $\frac{5}{8}$". Precut quilling papers come in many different solid, two-toned, or graduated colors; and are also available with gilded edges or a pearlized finish. Some craft stores carry a few basic quilling strips, but the best selection can be found on the Internet or by mail order. Several quilling supply resources are listed on page 124.

Note: Quilling papers are available by both English and American standards. English papers are 17" in length, while American papers are 23"–24". Color names and corresponding numbers are standard in the quilling industry.

English Colors

810 Pale Peach	816 Maize	819 Forest Green	821 Leaf Green	830 Pale Green
838 Pale Blue	843 Lilac	847 Rose Pink	853 Beech Brown	855 Robin Brown
858 Fawn	864 Light Gray	872 Oxford Blue	873 Lincoln Green	877 White/Silver Gilded Edge
877 White/Gold Gilded Edge	954 Navy	955 Burgundy	956 Lichen Green	958 Garnet
Brown and Rust	Dark Green and Light Green	Dark Yellow and Light Yellow	Orange and Light Yellow	Red and Light Orange

American Colors

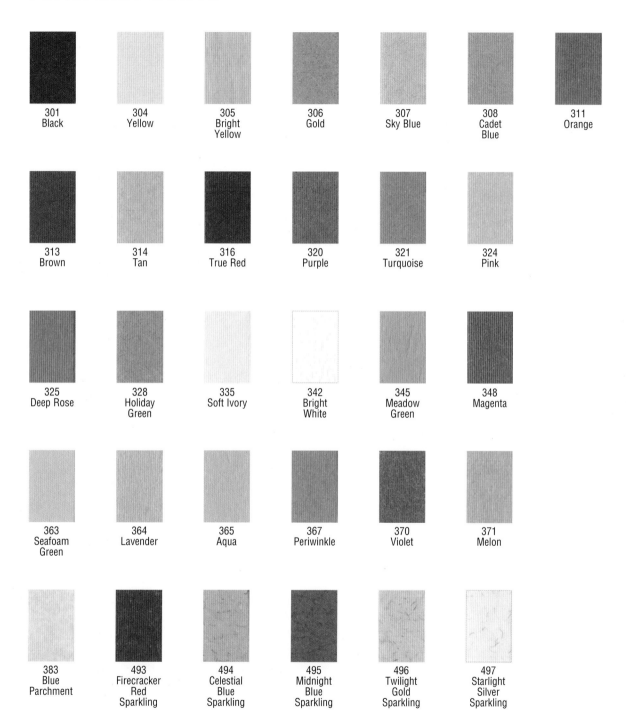

301 Black	304 Yellow	305 Bright Yellow	306 Gold	307 Sky Blue	308 Cadet Blue	311 Orange
313 Brown	314 Tan	316 True Red	320 Purple	321 Turquoise	324 Pink	
325 Deep Rose	328 Holiday Green	335 Soft Ivory	342 Bright White	345 Meadow Green	348 Magenta	
363 Seafoam Green	364 Lavender	365 Aqua	367 Periwinkle	370 Violet	371 Melon	
383 Blue Parchment	493 Firecracker Red Sparkling	494 Celestial Blue Sparkling	495 Midnight Blue Sparkling	496 Twilight Gold Sparkling	497 Starlight Silver Sparkling	

You can cut your own ¹/₁₆"-wide quilling papers from ⅛"-wide strips with the help of steady hands and a good pair of scissors. Simply cut the ⅛"-wide strips in half lengthwise from desired colors. This is helpful in avoiding a trip to the craft store or a lengthy wait for an online order.

Precut quilling paper is preferable because it is most precise; but if obtaining it proves difficult, you also have the option to cut your own. Medium-weight paper, somewhere between typing paper (20 lb.) and cardstock (67 lb.) is best. Typing paper is all right for small circles and shapes, but is generally too loose and makes limp scrolls. Cardstock leaves bumps if cut against the grain and makes heavy-looking shapes. To cut the strips as close to the same width as possible, a good paper cutter, such as a 12" rotary, is necessary.

Suggestion:

Construction paper is an inexpensive choice when quilling with school children. A quick way to cut quilling strips from construction paper is to run it through a paper shredder that makes ¹/₄"-wide strips. The projects in this book are not necessarily designed for children, but with a little instruction and guidance from the teacher, they can make their own creative handiwork.

Quilling tools: Ideally, quilling should be done on either a slotted or a needle tool. These tools are made specifically for quilling and are very economical (about $10 US for the set of two.)

The slotted tool has an opening at the top into which the quilling paper is inserted. This slot holds the paper in place while the strip is rolled around the tool. I recommend this tool for beginners because it makes quilling less frustrating. The small drawback to the slotted tool is that the centers of quilled shapes turn out some-what large with a section that does not curl; however, most people do not even notice this when looking at a completed design.

The needle tool gives quilled shapes a very compact center and is especially useful for rolling tight circles and spirals. It can be frustrating for beginners to use because it doesn't hold the strip in place by itself and is more difficult to get started. However, with some practice and patience, it oftentimes becomes the quiller's tool of choice.

If quilling tools are not available, a straight pin or round toothpick can be used. Much like the needle tool, a straight pin gives shapes a tight center, while a toothpick creates larger ones.

Suggestion:

Toothpicks work well when quilling with a group of school children as an inexpensive alternative.

Ruler: A ruler of any type can be used as long as it is 6"–12" long, or metric equivalent. The ruler is used to measure and tear the strips to the appropriate lengths for a particular shape to be quilled.

Additional Supplies

The following supplies are not necessary but are suggested to help make quilling easier and more professional looking. These items are used in many of the projects in this book, so I recommend you have them ready for use.

Graph paper: Graph paper helps keep quilling paper strips even while weaving. Graph paper with eight squares per inch is used for $1/8$"-wide strips while four squares per inch works for $1/4$"-wide weaves.

Paper crimper: A paper crimper gives quilling strips a zigzag look.

Quilling designer board: The quilling designer board is made of cork and is $5^3/4$" x $8^1/2$" in size.

One side of the board has a hard plastic template with 36 circles in six sizes. These circles are used to hold quilled strips of the same size in shape while the adhesive dries. There is also a small space on the board to hold other quilled shapes in place while drying. The back of the board doubles as a smaller version of a quilling work board.

Quilling work board: The quilling work board is an 8" x 10" corkboard used to hold quilled shapes in place with pins while the adhesive dries. Cover the board with waxed paper to prevent excess adhesive from sticking to the cork.

Suggestion:

A homemade version of the quilling work board can be fashioned from corrugated cardboard with one smooth side covered in waxed paper.

Scissors: Small, sharp, pointed scissors work best, generally used for creating fringed flowers or leaves.

Scratch paper: Scratch paper is used to trace provided patterns and templates.

Straight pins: Straight pins are used to hold quilled shapes together while the adhesive dries, or for rolling shapes such as tight circles.

Toothpick: A toothpick can be used to apply adhesive to quilled shapes.

Tweezers: Fine-tipped, preferably bent-nosed tweezers are used to pick up and position small shapes for adhering.

Waxed paper: Waxed paper is used on top of the quilling work board to keep the quilled shapes from sticking to the board once adhered.

Card and Scrapbook Page Supplies

In addition to the quilling supplies listed, some paper-crafting supplies are also necessary to make the cards and scrapbook pages in this book. Some of these supplies are used in only a few projects in this book, and may not be needed for the project(s) you choose to make.

Beads: Beads can be used to embellish a card or scrapbook page. Use an adhesive that will hold, so the beads do not fall off later on.

Bone folder: A bone folder creates crisp folded edges. A paper-cutter scoring-blade accessory will also work in place of a bone folder.

Cardstocks: Cardstocks come in two sizes: 8½" x 11" or 12" square. They are available in a wide variety of colors, many different weights, and with smooth or textured surfaces. Acid-free cardstocks will help protect photos used on scrapbook pages.

Chalks: Chalks are used to color the edges of cardstocks or quilled shapes. Use chalks that are manufactured specifically for paper.

Computer and color printer: Although not necessary, a computer word-processing program with various fonts, sizes, and colors, and a color printer are

helpful for creating some of the designs in this book. Heavy-weight cardstock will not fit in most printers, so check specifications before printing.

Corner edgers: Corner edgers have a slot into which paper is inserted to give corners decorative detail.

Corner rounder: This paper punch rounds out the corners of paper or cardstock for a softer look.

Cotton swabs: Cotton swabs are used to apply chalk to paper.

Decorative-edged scissors: The decorative blades of these scissors come in many styles and are manufactured by several companies.

Embossing ink pads: These ink pads hold specific inks used for heat embossing. Very light in color, embossing ink stays wet for a few minutes to allow embossing time. The ink is difficult to see after image has been stamped.

Embossing powders: Embossing powders stick to wet embossing ink. It is important not to accidentally rub off any of the powder before it has become permanent with the heat gun.

Eraser: Although any good eraser will work to erase pattern lines, a gum eraser (available in the craft-store art department) will also remove excess dried adhesive from paper.

Fabric ribbons: You can use any size, type, or color of fabric ribbon to add to your cards and scrapbook page designs. Use an adhesive that will hold so the ribbon does not fall off the cardstock or paper later on.

Heat gun: Use a heat gun to melt embossing powder applied to wet embossing ink, allowing it to become shiny. The heat gun is extremely hot, so use caution when holding cardstock or paper in place.

Ink pads: Ink pads are available in various sizes, colors, and types of ink, and are manufactured by many companies.

Markers: Markers come in many colors and styles and are used for writing, drawing lines and dots, or for coloring in letters or stencils. They can also be used to apply color to rubber stamps. The ink must be moistened first by exhaling, or "huffing," on the stamp; otherwise, it will be too dry and result in a poorly stamped image.

Mulberry papers: Mulberry papers are similar to heavy tissue papers, with strands of fiber running through them. The edges look great when wetted and torn.

Papers: Papers come in two sizes: 8½" x 11" and 12" square. The projects in this book call for various types of paper, so it is helpful to have a good supply of various colors, patterns, and surface finishes. Use acid-free papers for photo protection.

Paper cutters: There are many types and sizes of paper cutters available. The 12" rotary is large enough to trim 12"-square paper, is accurate and neat, and can also be used for cutting quilling strips. However, many types of paper cutters can be used, so try what you already have before investing in a new one. A scoring-blade accessory is also helpful for scoring cardstock when making cards.

Paper punches: Paper punches come in many shapes and sizes. They are used to punch out shapes from cardstock and paper to adhere to your cards and scrapbook pages.

Paper ribbons: Paper ribbons actually look like paper lace and may be called that instead of paper ribbon. They come in several colors and sizes.

Pencil: A sharp pencil is used for tracing templates. Trace shape on the back of the cardstock or paper, or erase all pencil lines for a more professional look.

Rubber stamps: Hundreds, if not thousands, of rubber stamps in various sizes and styles with words and images are available from many manufacturers.

Rub-ons: These are words or images printed on a sheet and transferred to another surface by rubbing them on.

Sponge daubers: Round sponges are mounted on plastic tubes that fit on fingertips. Sponge daubers are used to apply ink to cardstock or paper, usually through a stencil or template opening.

Sponges: Sponges are used to apply ink to cardstock or paper. Use a sponge that is manufactured for ink and paper use. Sponges also can be used to wet the edges of paper or cardstock before tearing.

Stencils and templates: Stencils and templates are used for marking and cutting out shapes from cardstock, paper, and photos. They are also used to mark letters on cardstock and paper. If the letters are to be cut out, mark the back of the cardstock or paper so the pencil marks will not need to be erased. Many sizes and styles of stencils and templates are available to choose from.

Stickers: There are many acid-free stickers available for use with paper.

Vellum paper: Similar to parchment paper, vellum gives a translucent look to the paper underneath, and adds a nice soft touch to any project.

Vellum tape: Made specifically for adhering vellum to paper and cardstock, vellum tape is hardly noticeable.

Water brush: This is a handy gadget to have for wetting the edges of paper or cardstock before tearing. The brush holds and carefully dispenses water where needed.

Techniques
Quilling Techniques

Quilling generally consists of rolling a length of narrow paper and manipulating it into a specific shape. Sometimes the end of the rolled strip is adhered, sometimes left loose. The quilled shapes outlined here are ones that have been used for designs in this book, but are not the only ones that exist in quilling.

An important point to remember when beginning quilling is to have clean, dry hands. Quilling paper does not roll if it gets wet, nor do shapes look good if dirty.

Most often, the quilling paper should be torn to the specified length before rolling it on the appropriate quilling tool. This torn end is less noticeable when adhered than if the strip was cut. However, sometimes it is preferable to cut the quilling paper instead of tearing it. The instructions in this book will specify if the strip should be cut instead of torn, thus familiarizing you with different looks.

Most of the shapes in this book are rolled on the slotted quilling tool. The tight circle and grape roll should be quilled on the needle tool rather than on a slotted quilling tool for best results. However, the other quilled shapes below can be quilled successfully with either tool. I have made most of the quilled designs in this book with the slotted tool because it is easier to manipulate than the needle tool. When the shape should be rolled on the needle tool, I have specified that in the instructions.

If this is your first time paper quilling, practice making some of these shapes before attempting the designs in this book. Relax, have fun, and be patient: you may be amazed at the results of this enjoyable art form. Welcome to the art of paper quilling.

Quilled Rolls

Tight circle: Tear specified length from quilling paper and slightly moisten end of strip against lips. Using needle tool or straight pin and beginning with moistened end of strip, roll strip around tool with thumb and index finger, keeping edges even. Slip rolled strip off of tool and adhere end. Hold for about ten seconds so adhesive grabs well and roll does not unwind. *Note: It may help to "curl" beginning end of strip before wetting, by pulling gently between needle tool and thumb.*

Suggestion:

If edges of strip are not even, set tight circle on work board surface and press down with finger or nail.

Grape roll: Roll and adhere a tight circle. Push up on center to form a cone shape, and spread adhesive inside to hold.

Loose circle: Roll a tight circle on a quilling tool. Allow circle to expand to desired size. Adhere end and place in appropriate circle template on quilling  designer board, if available. Adjust as necessary to fit template space. This is the basis for many of the other shapes, which are formed by pinching and squeezing loose circles in various ways.

Quilled Shapes

Teardrop: Roll a loose circle and adhere end. Pinch point at adhered edge of circle or opposite adhered edge, depending on where the  shapes will be joined together so end is least noticeable.

Marquise: Roll a loose circle and adhere end. Pinch two points into circle: one at adhered edge and one directly opposite.

Triangle: Roll a loose circle and adhere end. Pinch into teardrop shape, then press  rounded end against finger to form two more points. If no lengths are given, triangle will have three equal sides; when provided, two sides should be pinched to specified lengths.

Square: Roll a loose circle and adhere end. Form a marquise and turn 90°.  Pinch remaining sides to form four points and four equal sides.

Rectangle: Roll a loose circle and adhere end. Form a marquise, and pinch remaining sides into points at speci-  fied distance from first points for proper length.

Diamond: Roll a loose circle and adhere end. Pinch into a square, but pinch two points tighter than oppo- 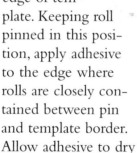 site two points to elongate.

Half circle: Roll a loose circle and adhere end. Form a teardrop, and  pinch second point at specified distance from first, to form flat base of half circle.

Bunny ears: Roll a loose cir-  cle and adhere end. Hold circle between thumb and index finger and push one edge of circle in to form two points, or bunny ears, on circle.

Eccentric shapes: Many of the rolled shapes can be made into an eccentric shape. Begin with an adhered loose circle contained within the appropriately sized template on  the quilling designer board. Insert straight pin into inner- most roll and pull center to edge of tem- plate. Keeping roll  pinned in this posi- tion, apply adhesive to the edge where rolls are closely con- 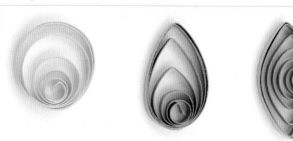 tained between pin and template border. Allow adhesive to dry before removing and pinching into desired shape.

Spiral: Cut or tear specified length of quilling paper needed. Place strip at an angle near tip of needle tool. Keeping strip taut, roll around tool at an angle, allowing spiral to slide up and off tip of tool until you reach other end of strip. Tighten or loosen spiral as needed.

Note: Strip can be rolled around tool in opposite direction to form mirror image spirals.

Folded rose: Roll 6" strip of $\frac{1}{4}$"-wide quilling paper a few turns on slotted tool. Fold strip back at a right angle, continuing to roll. Keep bottom edges straight, and allow strip to flair out at top edge. Repeat folding and rolling every few turns until end of strip is reached. Trim as needed and adhere end. Remove from tool and apply adhesive to base of petals to prevent unrolling; hold

or pin until dry.

Fringed flower: Use specified length of $\frac{1}{4}$"-wide or $\frac{3}{8}$"-wide quilling paper, cardstock, or regular paper. Cut slits $\frac{1}{16}$" apart along top edge of strip, leaving a $\frac{1}{16}$" base. Roll uncut edge on needle tool and adhere end. Fringes can be left tight or spread apart with fingers.

Fringed Flower with contrasting center: Cut slits as per fringed flower in specified length of $\frac{1}{4}$"-wide or $\frac{3}{8}$"-wide quilling paper, cardstock, or regular paper. Contrasting color of specified length should be $\frac{1}{16}$" wide. Adhere ends of contrasting strips together, overlapping slightly. Roll on needle tool, beginning with $\frac{1}{16}$"-wide strip. Adhere end. Spread fringes apart to reveal contrasting center.

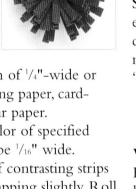

Quilled Scrolls:

Scroll: Tear necessary length from quilling paper. Roll one end far enough that finished scroll is specified length, if given.

C-scroll: Roll each end toward middle to form "C" shape.

S-scroll: Roll each end in opposite directions toward middle to form "S" shape.

V-scroll: Fold strip in half. Roll each end outward toward fold.

Heart: Fold strip in half. Roll ends inward. Adhere between rolls, unless instructions say to leave open.

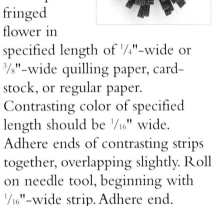

Quilled Alphabet

General Instructions:

- Roll strips ⁵⁄₈" on each end for ³⁄₄"-tall letters. Roll slightly less for ⁷⁄₈"-tall letters. Adjust any rolled lengths as necessary to achieve desired letter height.

- To curve middle of strip, hold one end of strip. Beginning at held end, pull strip between edge of quilling tool and finger of other hand.

- Adhere rolled strips together as shown in diagrams and photographs.

- Adjust strips as needed with fingers or quilling tool after rolling strips.

Uppercase Letters:

A: Begin with a 3" V-scroll. Roll ends ⁵⁄₈" outward. Roll a 1" C-scroll, allowing ends to meet. Adhere rolls of C-scroll together.

B: Roll ends of three 2" strips ⁵⁄₈". Leave one strip as is; curve middle of remaining strips inward to form "C" shape.

C: Roll ends of a 3" strip ⁵⁄₈"; curve middle to form "C" shape.

D: Roll ends of a 2" strip ⁵⁄₈". Roll ends of a 2¹⁄₂" strip ⁵⁄₈" and curve middle.

E: Roll ends of a 2" strip ⁵⁄₈". Fold two 2¹⁄₂" strips at 1" and 1³⁄₈" for ³⁄₄"-tall letters. Roll each end ⁵⁄₈" inward. For ⁷⁄₈"-tall letters, fold one 2¹⁄₂" strip at 1" and 1³⁄₈" and one 2¹⁄₂" strip at ⁷⁄₈" and 1³⁄₈".

F: Roll ends of a 2" strip ⁵⁄₈". Fold a 2¹⁄₂" strip at 1" and 1³⁄₈". Roll each end ⁵⁄₈" inward.

G: Roll ends of a 3" strip ⁵⁄₈" and curve middle inward. Roll ends of a 1¹⁄₂" strip to measure ³⁄₈" long.

H: Roll ends of two 2" strips ⁵⁄₈". Roll a 1¹⁄₂" C-scroll, allowing ends to meet. Adhere rolls together.

I: Fold two 2¹⁄₂" strips at ⁷⁄₈" and 1⁵⁄₈" for ³⁄₄"-tall letters or at ⁷⁄₈" and 1³⁄₄" for ⁷⁄₈"-tall letters. Roll ends ¹⁄₂" to ⁵⁄₈", so that fold to end of roll measures ¹⁄₄".

J: Roll one end of a 2" strip ⁵⁄₈", curving rolled end inward ⁵⁄₈" from straight end, and stopping at roll. Roll ends of a 2" strip ⁵⁄₈" to ³⁄₄" to measure ⁵⁄₈"-long.

K: Roll ends of a 2" strip ⁵⁄₈". Fold a 2¹⁄₂" strip in half; roll ¹⁄₂"–⁵⁄₈" on each end inward.

L: Fold a 2¹⁄₂" strip at 1". Roll long end ⁵⁄₈"–³⁄₄" outward and short end ¹⁄₂" inward.

M: Begin with a 2¹⁄₂" V-scroll. Roll ends ⁵⁄₈" outward. Roll one end of two 1¹⁄₂" strips ⁵⁄₈"–³⁄₄".

N: Roll ends of a 2¹⁄₂" strip ⁵⁄₈"–³⁄₄" in opposite directions. Roll one end of two 1¹⁄₂" strips ⁵⁄₈"–³⁄₄".

O: Roll one end of a 3" strip ⁵⁄₈". Curve remainder of strip inward and adhere in "O" shape.

P: Roll ends of two 2" strips ⁵⁄₈". Curve middle of one strip inward to form "C" shape.

Q: Roll one end of a 3" strip ⁵⁄₈". Curve remainder of strip inward, and adhere in "O" shape. Quill 1" loose circle; adhere to rolled side of "O".

R: Roll ends of two 2" strips ⁵⁄₈". Curve middle of one strip inward to form "C" shape. Roll one end of a 1¹⁄₄" strip ⁵⁄₈"–³⁄₄".

S: Roll ends of a 3¹⁄₂" strip ⁵⁄₈" in opposite directions. Curve each half of strip inward from center to roll.

T: Fold two 2¹⁄₄" strips ⁷⁄₈" from one end. Roll ends ¹⁄₂" inward.

U: Roll ends of a 3" strip ¹⁄₂"–⁵⁄₈"; curve middle 1" of strip outward.

V: Begin with a 3" V-scroll; roll ends ⁵⁄₈" outward.

W: Fold two 2¹⁄₂" strips 1" from one end. Roll ¹⁄₂"–⁵⁄₈" on short end inward and ¹⁄₂"–⁵⁄₈" on long end outward.

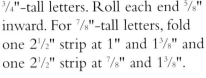
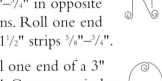

X: Begin with two 2" V-scrolls. Roll ends ¹/₂"–⁵/₈" outward.

Y: Fold two 2" strips in half and roll ends ¹/₂"–⁵/₈" inward.

Z: Fold a 3¹/₂" strip 1¹/₄" from each end in opposite directions. Roll each end ⁵/₈" inward.

Lowercase Letters:

a: Roll ends of a 2¹/₄" strip ⁵/₈" and curve middle inward. Roll ends of a 1¹/₂" strip ⁵/₈".

b: Roll ends of a 2¹/₄" strip ⁵/₈" and curve middle inward. Roll ends of a 2" strip ⁵/₈".

c: Roll ends of a 2¹/₄" strip ⁵/₈" and curve middle inward.

d: Roll ends of a 2¹/₄" strip ⁵/₈"and curve middle inward. Roll ends of a 2" strip ⁵/₈".

e: Fold a 3" strip at 1". Curve long end inward. Roll each end ⁵/₈" inward.

f: Fold a 2" strip at ⁷/₈". Roll each end ⁵/₈" inward. Fold a 2" strip at ⁷/₈". Curve long end inward. Roll ⁵/₈" on long end inward and ⁵/₈" on short end outward.

g: Roll ends of a 2¹/₂" strip ⁵/₈" in opposite directions. Curve one end inward from center to roll. Roll a 2¹/₄" strip ⁵/₈" on each end and curve middle inward.

h: Roll ends of a 2" strip ⁵/₈". Roll a 1¹/₂" strip ⁵/₈" on one end and ³/₈" on other end, in opposite directions. Curve inward toward ³/₈" roll.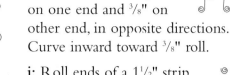

i: Roll ends of a 1¹/₂" strip ⁵/₈" in opposite directions. Quill a 1" loose circle.

j: Roll ends of a 2¹/₂" strip ⁵/₈" in opposite directions. Curve one end inward from center to roll. Quill 1" loose circle.

k: Roll a 2" strip ⁵/₈" on each end. Fold a 1³/₄" strip in half and roll ⁵/₈" on each end inward.

l: Roll a 2" strip ⁵/₈" on each end in opposite directions.

m: Roll ends of a 1¹/₂" strip ⁵/₈". Roll one end of two 1¹/₂" strips ⁵/₈", and ³/₈" on other end in opposite directions. Curve inward toward ³/₈" roll.

n: Roll ends of a 1¹/₂" strip ⁵/₈". Roll one end of a 1¹/₂" strip ⁵/₈" and other end ³/₈" in opposite directions. Curve inward toward ³/₈" roll.

o: Roll one end of a 2" strip ⁵/₈". Curve remainder of strip inward to form "O" shape.

p: Roll ends of a 2" strip ⁵/₈". Roll ends of a 2¹/₄" strip ⁵/₈" and curve middle inward.

q: Roll ends of a 2¹/₄" strip ⁵/₈" and curve middle inward. Roll ends of a 2¹/₄" strip ⁵/₈". Curve one end ³/₈" inward.

r: Roll ends of a 1¹/₂" strip ⁵/₈". Roll a 1" strip ⁵/₈" on one end; curve remainder of strip slightly inward.

s: Roll ends of a 2¹/₂" strip ⁵/₈" in opposite directions. Curve each half of strip inward from center to roll.

t: Fold a 2" strip at ⁷/₈". Roll ⁵/₈" on short end inward and ⁵/₈" on long end outward. Roll ends of a 1³/₄" V-scroll ⁵/₈" outward.

u: Curve middle 1" of a 2¹/₂" strip. Roll ends ¹/₂"–⁵/₈" outward.

v: Roll ends of a 2¹/₄" V-scroll ⁵/₈" outward.

w: Fold two 2" strips ⁷/₈" from one end. Roll short end ⁵/₈" inward and long end ⁵/₈" outward.

x: Roll ends of two 1¹/₂" V-scrolls ¹/₂"–⁵/₈" outward.

y: Roll ends of a 2¹/₂" strip ⁵/₈" in opposite directions. Curve one end inward from center to roll. Roll one end of a 1¹/₂" strip ⁵/₈". Roll other end ³/₈" in opposite direction. Curve inward toward ³/₈" roll.

z: Fold a 2⁵/₈" strip 1" from each end in opposite directions. Roll ends ⁵/₈" inward.

Quilled Numbers

0: Roll one end of a 3" strip ⅝". Curve remainder of strip inward.

1: Fold a 1¾" strip in half. Roll one end ⅝" outward.

2: Fold a 3" strip at 1". Roll short end ⅝" inward and long end ⅝" outward. Curve long end outward and slightly adhere fold.

3: Fold a 3¼" strip in half. Roll ends ⅝" outward. Curve outward from fold to each end. Slightly adhere fold.

4: Fold a 2" strip ⅞" from each end. Roll ends ⅝" outward. Fold a 1½" strip at ½". Roll short end ⅜" inward and long end ⅝" outward. Adhere strips together.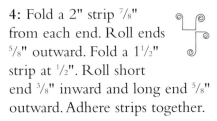

5: Fold a 3" strip at 1" and 1⅜". Roll short end ⅝" inward and long end ⅝" outward. Curve long end outward from fold to roll.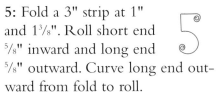

6: Roll ends of a 3½" strip ⅝". Curve middle of strip inward.

7: Fold a 2½" strip at 1⅛". Roll short end ⅝" inward and long end ⅝" outward.

8: Roll two 2" strips ⅝" on one end. Curve remainder of strip inward. Adhere strips together.

9: Roll ends of a 3½" strip ⅝". Curve middle of strip inward.

24

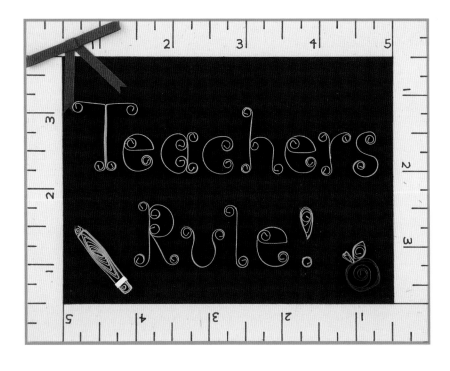

Quilled Punctuation Marks

Period: Quill a 1" loose circle.

Comma/apostrophe: Roll one end of a 1" strip ⅝".

Exclamation point: Quill a 4½" teardrop and a 1" loose circle.

Question mark: Fold a 1⅝" strip at ⅛". Roll long end ⅝" outward. Curve long end outward from fold to roll. Quill a 1" loose circle.

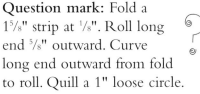

Lowercase Alphabet, Punctuation & Numbers

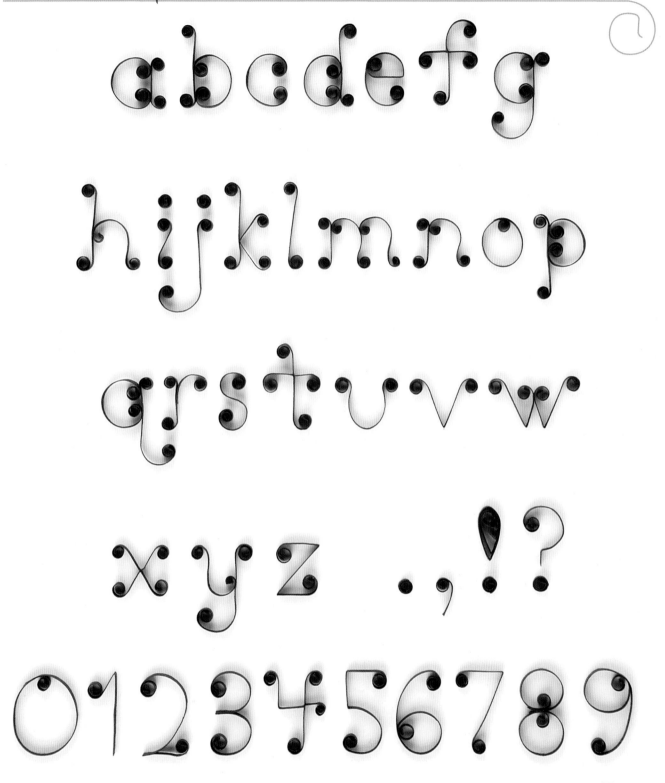

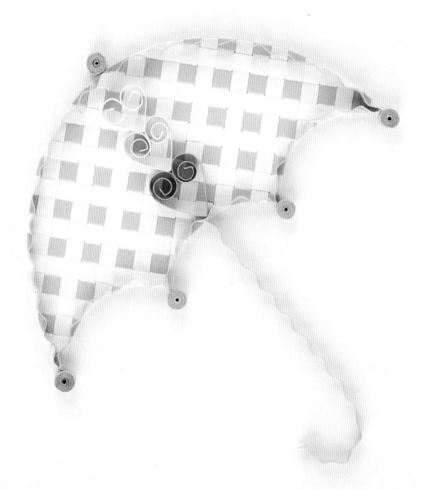

Bridal Shower

2

Quilled Cards

All of the cards in this book are either 5¹⁄₂" x 4¹⁄₄" or 6¹⁄₂" x 5" to fit in readily available envelopes. Larger, padded envelopes can be used to protect quilled cards when sending them in the mail. Because of personal color preferences or a lack of supplies, you may want to change the colors of cardstock, paper, quilling papers, or other supplies used for these card designs.

Wedding Invitation

This card can be given with a wedding gift or used as an invitation.

Finished Size: 6½" x 5"

Quilling Materials:

Note: Refer to Quilling Tools and Supplies on pages 12–15.

- ⅛"-wide quilling papers:

    Bright white
    Soft ivory

- ¼"-wide quilling paper:

    Bright white

- ¹⁄₁₆"-wide quilling paper:

    Soft ivory

- Cardstock:

    Ivory: (3) ½" x ¼"

Quilling Instructions:

Note: Refer to Quilling Techniques on pages 18–25.

Rose: Quill white folded rose, using 6" strip of ¼"-wide quilling paper.

Fringed flower (make 2): Quill fringed flower with contrasting center, using white 3" length of ¼"-wide strip and ivory 1" length of ¹⁄₁₆"-wide strip.

Scroll (make 3): Roll and curve ivory 2" length of ⅛"-wide strip to be about 1" long.

Leaf (make 3): Fold ivory ½" x ¼" cardstock in half lengthwise. Cut out leaf shape.

Cut angled slits from outer edge of leaf toward fold, stopping ¹⁄₁₆" from fold. Unfold leaf.

Ribbon: Cut white 16" length of ⅛"-wide quilling paper. Curve two loops about 4" from one end of strip.

Card Materials:

- Cardstocks:

    Ivory: 3¼" x 2¼"
    White: 10" x 6½", 3" x 2"

- Papers:

    Vellum: 10" x 6½"
    White/ivory rose print: 6½" x 5"

- Decorative-edged scissors: mini-scallop

- Embossing ink pad

- Embossing powders: gold, white

- Heat gun

- Rubber stamps: "To Love and To Cherish", rose border

- Vellum tape

Card Instructions:

Score and fold 10" x 6½" cardstock to form card.

Adhere rose print paper to front of card.

Fold vellum in half. Stamp and emboss rose border to bottom front of vellum with embossing powder.

Trim bottom edge of vellum with decorative-edged scissors. Adhere vellum to card with vellum tape.

Trim edges of ivory and remaining white cardstock with decorative-edged scissors. Layer and adhere cardstock pieces to card as shown in photograph, or as desired. Stamp and emboss "To Love and To Cherish."

Adhere ribbon loops to card. Trim as needed and cut notches in ends. Twist and adhere strips as shown.

Arrange and adhere rose, fringed flowers, scrolls, and leaves on top of ribbon loops.

Suggestion:

If using the card as a wedding invitation, make color copies of one card to save time quilling many.

Invitation

This invitation can be used for almost any occasion. To make it less formal, omit the cadet blue tight circles.

Finished Size: 5½" x 4¼"

Quilling Materials:

Note: Refer to Quilling Tools and Supplies on pages 12–15.

- ⅛"-wide quilling papers:
    Cadet blue
    Navy

Quilling Instructions:

Note: Refer to Quilling Techniques on pages 18–25.

Quill sixteen 2½" navy S-scrolls. Loosen rolls and shape scrolls to ¾" long.

Quill two 2½" navy V-scrolls. Loosen rolls and shape scrolls to ¾" long.

Quill thirty-six 1" cadet blue tight circles.

Quill fourteen 1" cadet blue teardrops.

Quill four 1" navy teardrops.

Card Materials:

- Cardstocks:
    Dark blue: 5¼" x 4", 4" x 2¾"
    Light blue: 5" x 3¾"
    White: 11" x 8½"
- Computer/color printer or marker

Card Instructions:

Print "You Are Invited" on 11" x 8½" cardstock. *Note: If computer and printer are not available, hand-print words with marker. Evenly trim to 3¾" x 2½".*

Cut remaining white cardstock to 8½" x 5½"; score and fold to form card.

Center and adhere cardstock to card as shown in photograph, or as desired. Adhere quote trim to card.

Arrange and adhere quilled shapes to front of card as shown.

Baby or Bridal Shower Invitation

Baby or Bridal Shower Invitation

This card can be designed for a baby or bridal shower. Simply choose wording to correspond with your upcoming event.

Note: If making this card for a baby shower, simply choose three colors of quilling strips and substitute for those used in woven umbrella instructions.
Finished Size: 4¼" x 5½"

Quilling Materials:

Note: Refer to Quilling Tools and Supplies on pages 12–15.

(Suggested colors for bridal shower)

- ⅛"-wide quilling papers in three colors:

    Ivory

    Tan

    White

(Suggested colors for baby shower)

- ⅛"-wide quilling papers

    Bright white

    Maize

    Pale blue

    Pale green

    Pink

- Graph paper

- Paper crimper

- Scratch paper

Quilling Instructions:

Note: Refer to Quilling Techniques on pages 18–25.

Woven umbrella: Tear twenty-two 3" ivory, ten 3" tan, and ten 3" white strips. Use graph paper to keep strips straight and at right angles. Place one tan strip horizontally along graph paper. Adhere top edges of ivory strips perpendicularly to tan strip, alternating over and under. Do not overlap strips. (See Figs. 1A & 1B)

Turn graph paper 180°. Weave a white strip parallel to tan strip, alternating over and under ivory strip opposite where tan is weaved.

Slide newly woven strip down with fingernails to snugly fit next to previous strip. Lift up vertical strips and place a tiny drop of adhesive to adhere horizontal strip. Continue weaving and adhering, alternating tan and white strips one at a time. (See Fig. 1C) *Note: Once all strips have been used, woven piece should measure approximately 3"-square.*

Trace Woven Umbrella Template onto scratch paper and cut out. Place template diagonally over woven section. Trace and cut out. Adhere any loose edges.

Crimp 15" tan strip. Adhere edge of crimped strip to edges of woven umbrella.

Cut crimped strip at each umbrella point and use separate crimped sections for each curve. Cut 2½" length of crimped strip and shape into umbrella handle.

Quill five 3" tan tight circles with needle tool.

Quill 3" tan heart, 2½" ivory heart, and 2" white heart. Arrange and adhere handle, tight circles, and hearts to umbrella as shown in photograph.

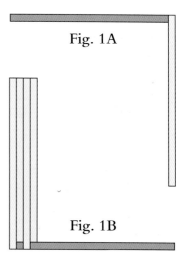

Fig. 1A

Fig. 1B

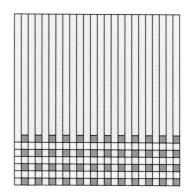

Fig. 1C

Card Materials:

(Suggested colors for bridal shower)

• Cardstocks:

    Ivory: 5" x 3³/₄"
    Tan: 5¹/₄" x 4", 3" x 1"
    White: 11" x 8¹/₂"

(Suggested colors for baby shower)

• Cardstocks:

    Blue: 3" x 1"
    Pink: 5¹/₄" x 4"
    White: 11" x 8¹/₂",
    5" x 3³/₄"

• Computer/color printer or marker

• Corner edgers

• Corner rounder

Card Instructions:

Print "Bridal Shower" or "Baby Shower" on 11" x 8¹/₂" cardstock.

Note: If computer and printer are not available, hand-print words with marker.

Evenly trim to 2³/₄" x ³/₄" and round corners. Layer and adhere to 3" x 1" cardstock. Round corners.

Cut remaining 11" x 8¹/₂" card-stock down to 8¹/₂" x 5¹/₂"; score and fold to form card. Round corners.

Use corner edgers on remaining cardstock. Layer and adhere to front of card as shown in photograph.

Arrange and adhere wording and umbrella piece to front of card.

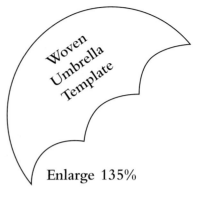

Woven Umbrella Template

Enlarge 135%

New Baby Card

This card can be used as a baby gift card, baby shower invitation, or birth announcement.

Finished Size: 5½" x 4¼"

Quilling Materials:

Note: Refer to Quilling Tools and Supplies on pages 12–15.

(Suggested colors for baby boy)

• ⅛"-wide quilling papers:

Cadet blue
Lavender
Pink
Seafoam green
Yellow

(Suggested colors for baby girl)

• ⅛"-wide quilling papers:

Cadet blue
Deep Rose
Lavender
Pink
Seafoam green
Yellow

Quilling Instructions:

Note: Refer to Quilling Techniques on pages 18–25.

Quill two pink or cadet blue 2" hearts.

Quill ¾"-tall cadet blue or rose "BABY."

Foot (make 2): Quill one yellow or lavender 6" loose circle. Squeeze bottom third to shape arch of foot.

Adhere rolls together inside indentation; pin until dry.

Quill one 1" and four ½" tight circles in corresponding color for toes.

Pacifier: Quill 4" green marquise. Quill 2" green loose circle; insert quilling tool in center and further loosen rolls.

Quill 3" yellow or lavender teardrop. Pinch a second point ⅛" from first point.

Adhere flat section of teardrop to one curved side of marquise. Adhere loose circle to opposite side of marquise.

Rattle: Quill 4" pink or cadet blue loose circle.

Quill 2" green loose circle. Insert quilling tool in center of loose circle and further loosen rolls.

Adhere ¼" green strip between circles to form handle.

Card Materials:

(Suggested colors for baby boy)

• Cardstocks:

Light blue: 5¼" x 4"
Medium blue: (4) 1⅛" x ⅞", (2) ⅞"-square
White: 8½" x 5½", (4) 1" x ¾", (2) ¾"-square

(Suggested colors for baby girl)

• Cardstocks:

Light pink: 5¼" x 4"
Medium pink: (2) ⅞"-square
Rose: (4) 1⅛" x ⅞"
White: 8½" x 5½", (4) 1" x ¾", (2) ¾"-square

Card Instructions:

Score and fold 8½" x 5½" cardstock to form card.

Layer, center, and adhere cardstock pieces to front of card as shown in photograph, or as desired.

Arrange and adhere quilled letters, feet, toes, pacifier, and rattle to front of card as shown, or as desired.

Thank You Card

Finished Size: 5½" x 4¼"

Quilling Materials:

Note: Refer to Quilling Tools and Supplies on pages 12–15.

- ⅛"-wide quilling papers:
    Aqua
    Bright yellow
    Lavender
    Magenta
    Meadow green
    Orange
    Pink
    Purple
    Turquoise
- ¹⁄₁₆"-wide quilling papers:
    Aqua
    Magenta
    Orange
- Cardstock:
    Dark green: (2) 1" x ½"
- Paper:
    Yellow: 3" x ¼"

Quilling Instructions:

Note: Refer to Quilling Techniques on pages 18–25.

Large daisy: Quill five 3" yellow teardrops.

Quill 2½" orange tight circle from ¹⁄₁₆"-wide quilling paper.

Adhere teardrops together with points in center. Adhere tight circle on top of center.

Large forget-me-not: Quill four 3" turquoise bunny ears.

Quill 3" aqua tight circle from ¹⁄₁₆"-wide quilling paper.

Adhere bunny ears together with curves in center. Adhere tight circle on top of center.

Fringed flower: Quill fringed flower with contrasting center, using 3" x ¼" yellow paper and 1" magenta ¹⁄₁₆"-wide strip.

Scroll (make 5): Roll and curve 1½" green strip to approximately ⅝" long.

Bud: Quill 3" magenta marquise.

Quill 1½" green V-scroll.

Adhere marquise to folded center of V-scroll. Adhere edge of V-scroll to edge of one scroll.

Round flower: Quill 5" yellow loose circle. Insert quilling tool in center and further loosen rolls.

Quill 1½" orange tight circle. Insert and adhere tight circle into center of loose circle.

Make six more round flowers in same manner, using 4" yellow loose circle with 1½" orange tight circle, 4" orange loose circle with 1½" yellow tight circle, 4" purple loose circle with 1½" lavender tight circle, 4" turquoise loose circle with 1½" aqua tight circle, and two 4" magenta loose circles with two 1½" pink tight circles.

Small leaf (make 14): Quill 2" green loose circle. Pinch in two spots about ⅛" apart and curve slightly between pinches.

Adhere ⅛" curved section of two leaves to edge of each round flower.

Large leaf (make 2): Fold 1" x ½" dark green cardstock in half lengthwise. Cut out leaf shape.

Cut angled slits from outer edge of leaf toward fold, stopping ¹⁄₁₆" from fold.

Adhere leaves to back of large daisy and large forget-me-not.

Card Materials:

- Cardstocks:
    Dark green: 5¼" x 4", 4½" x 3"
    White: 11" x 8½"
- Paper:
    Light green: 5" x 3¾"
- Computer/color printer or marker
- Corner edgers
- Scratch paper

Card Instructions:

Print "Thank You" on 11" x 8½" cardstock. *Note: If computer and printer are not available, hand-print words with marker.*

Trace Oval Template on scratch paper and cut out. Center cut-out template over printed words. Trace and cut out.

Center and adhere word cutout to 4½"
x 3" cardstock; cut out, leaving a ⅛"
border.

Cut remaining 11" x 8½" cardstock to
8½" x 5½". Score and fold to form card.

Use corner edgers on 5¼" x 4" card–
stock and paper. Center and adhere to
card as shown in photograph, or as
desired.

Center and adhere word cutout to card.

Arrange and adhere flowers with attached
leaves and scrolls around oval as shown.

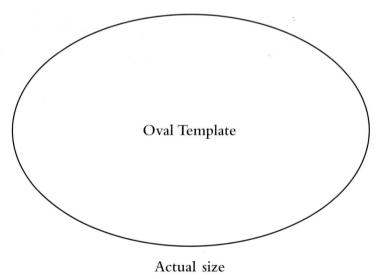

Oval Template

Actual size

Birthday Card

If the recipient of this card is having a first or second birthday, make only one or two candles to match their years.

Finished Size: 4¼" x 5½"

Quilling Materials:

Note: Refer to Quilling Tools and Supplies on pages 12–15.

- ⅛"-wide quilling papers:
    Bright yellow
    Holiday green
    True red
    Violet

Quilling Instructions:

Note: Refer to Quilling Techniques on pages 18–25.

Cake: Quill six yellow 12" squares. Adhere together in two rows of three.

Icing: Quill three red 3" S-scrolls

Quill four green 3" S-scrolls.

Candle (make 3):
Quill ³⁄₁₆" x ¾" rectangles from 9" strip violet quilling paper.

Quill 3" yellow teardrop for flame.

Adhere rounded end of flame to ³⁄₁₆" side of rectangle.

Adhere shapes together as shown in photograph.

Card Materials:

- Cardstocks:

    Dark blue: 4" x 5¼"
    White: 5½" x 8½" , 3¾" x 5"

- Corner rounder

- Ink pad: dark blue or desired color

- Rubber stamp: "Happy Birthday!"

Card Instructions:

Score and fold 5½" x 8½" cardstock to form card.

Round corners of card and cardstock pieces.

Stamp "Happy Birthday!" onto 3¾" x 5" cardstock, ³⁄₈" below top edge.

Cut ⅛" squares from quilling papers. Arrange and adhere as shown in photograph, or as desired.

Layer and adhere cardstock pieces to front of card as shown, or as desired.

Adhere cake below sentiment.

Suggestion:

A wider quilled cake can be made to accommodate more candles if desired. Simply quill two or four more squares, two or four more S-scrolls, and some extra candles.

Teacher Card

Finished Size: 5½" x 4¼"

Quilling Materials:

Note: Refer to Quilling Tools and Supplies on pages 12–15.

- ⅛"-wide quilling papers:
  - Bright yellow
  - Meadow green
  - Pink
  - Starlight silver sparkling
  - Tan
  - True red

Quilling Instructions:

Note: Refer to Quilling Techniques on pages 18–25.

Pencil: Quill ⅛" x ¹³/₁₆" rectangle from 9" yellow quilling strip.

Quill 1" tan triangle with needle tool.

Quill ⅛" x ³/₁₆" rectangle from 2" pink quilling strip with needle tool.

Adhere triangle and pink rectangle to opposite sides of yellow rectangle as shown in photograph. With black marker, color tip of triangle to resemble lead.

Cut 1" silver strip in half to ¹/₁₆"-wide. Adhere around quilled pencil where rectangles are joined; trim excess.

Apple: Quill 6" red loose circle. Indent top and bottom to form apple.

Quill 2" green marquise for leaf. Quill 1" green triangle with one ¹/₁₆" side and two ³/₁₆" sides for stem. Adhere leaf and stem to top of apple.

Bow: Cut 3" red strip. Adhere both ends to center of strip to form loops.

Wrap ½" red strip around center of loops and adhere. Trim excess.

Cut two 1" red strips for tails. Cut notch in one end of each strip.

Overlap and adhere other ends into a V-shape. Adhere overlap to center back of loops.

Letters: Quill ⅞"-tall uppercase and ½"-tall lowercase tan "Teachers Rule!"

Card Materials:

- Cardstocks:
  - Black: 4½" x 3¼"
  - Tan: 8½" x 5½"
- Marker: black

Card Instructions:

Score and fold 8½" x 5½" cardstock to form card.

Lightly mark ½" away from edges at corners in pencil. With black marker and ruler, draw line ½" from top edge, starting at left corner and stopping ½" from right corner. Turn card 90° to left and repeat for each side of card to form rulers as shown in photograph.

With pencil and ruler, mark every ¼" at edges on each side within each ruler section. Using black marker and ruler, mark ruler measurement lines starting at top left edge of card.
Note: Measurement lines should start at edge of card and should be ⅛"-long for quarter and three-quarter inches, ¼"-long for half inches, and ³/₈"-long for inches. Mark measurement lines all around edges of card until each ruler section is filled. Write inch numbers to left of each ³/₈"-long mark as shown in photograph.

Center and adhere remaining cardstock to front of card between rulers.

Arrange and adhere quilled letters, pencil, apple, and bow to front of card as shown, or as desired.

Graduation Card

Choose cardstock and quilling papers to match the graduating student's school colors.

Finished Size: $4^1/_4$" x $5^1/_2$"

Quilling Materials:

Note: Refer to Quilling Tools and Supplies on pages 12–15.

- $^1/_8$"-wide quilling papers:
    Navy
    Tan

Quilling Instructions:

Note: Refer to Quilling Techniques on pages 18–25.

Cap: Quill 18" navy diamond. Quill 15" navy uneven marquise with 1" side. Pinch shorter side halfway between previous pinches. Quill $^3/_4$" navy tight circle.

Adhere diamond shape on top of curved side of uneven marquise as shown in photograph. Adhere tight circle under top point of diamond to stabilize cap.

Tassel: Quill a fringed flower with 1" x $^1/_4$" tan cardstock; do not spread fringe.

Cut 1" tan quilling strip into one $^1/_{16}$"-wide strip and two $^1/_{32}$"-wide strips. Adhere one $^1/_{32}$"-wide strip around uncut end of rolled fringe. Trim as needed.

Trim remaining $^1/_{32}$"-wide strip down to $^3/_4$"-long. Adhere one end to inside center of uncut edge of rolled fringe. Adhere other end diagonally to center of diamond as shown in photograph.

Roll $^1/_{16}$"-wide strip into a tight circle. Adhere tight circle to center of diamond on top of adhered end of $^1/_{32}$"-wide strip.

Quill four tan 2" V-scrolls.

Card Materials:

- Cardstocks:

    Ivory: $8^1/_2$" x $5^1/_2$", 2"-square, $2^1/_2$" x $^5/_8$"

    Navy: $5^1/_4$" x 4", $2^3/_4$"-square, $2^1/_4$"-square, $2^3/_4$" x $^7/_8$"

    Tan: 3"-square, $2^1/_2$"-square, 1" x $^1/_4$"

    - Paper:

    Graduation print: 5" x $3^3/_4$"

- Corner rounder

- Marker: blue

- Rub-on sentiment: "We're so Proud"

Card Instructions:

Score and fold $8^1/_2$" x $5^1/_2$" cardstock to form card.

Round corners of card, desired cardstock, and graduation print paper.

Layer and adhere all cardstock to front of card as shown in photograph, or as desired.

Apply rub-on sentiment to front of card.

Draw dashed lines close to edges on sentiment strip and 2"-square cardstock with marker.

Adhere quilled pieces to card as shown, or as desired.

Suggestion:

Do not adhere left and right points of mounted diagonal squares, but tuck some rolled dollar bills beneath squares for a graduation gift.

We're so Proud

New Home Card

This card makes a nice accompaniment to a house-warming gift. It can also be used as an invitation to a house-warming party or to announce your new address by changing the quote trim to "Our New Home."

Finished Size: 4¼" x 5½"

Quilling Materials:

Note: Refer to Quilling Tools and Supplies on pages 12–15.

- ⅛"-wide quilling papers:

    Black
    Bright White
    Maize
    Pale green
    Pink
    Tan
    Turquoise

Quilling Instructions:

Note: Refer to Quilling Techniques on pages 18–25.

Cloud: Quill 15" white loose circle. Shape into cloud as desired.

Chimney: Quill 9" tan half circle with ⅜" base, using 6" hole on quilling designer board to make shape more dense. Pinch curve ¼" away from first points, so there are two parallel sides: one ⅜" long and one ⁹⁄₁₆" long. *Note: One ¼" end should be perpendicular to parallel sides while opposite ¼" end should be diagonal.*

Heart: Quill 2" pink heart.

Door: Quill 15" turquoise rectangle with two ⁵⁄₁₆" sides and two ¾" sides, using 12" hole on quilling designer board to make shape more dense.

Flower: Quill 3" pink loose circle. Insert quilling tool in center to further loosen rolls.

Quill 1½" maize tight circle. Insert and adhere tight circle in center of loose circle.

Cut ⅜" green strip for stem. Quill two 1½" green marquises with needle tool for leaves. Adhere one marquise on each side of stem base.

Card Materials:

- Cardstocks:

    Light blue: 5¼" x 4"
    Light gray: 1" x ¾"
    Light green: 4" x 1"
    Light yellow: 2½" x 2"
    White: 11" x 8½"

- Paper:

    Turquoise: 3⅝" x 1¼", (2) ⅜"-square

- Computer/color printer or marker

- Decorative-edged scissors: deckle

- Scratch paper

Card Instructions:

Print "Welcome to Your New Home" or desired quote on cardstock. *Note: If computer and printer are not available, hand-print words with marker.* Evenly trim to 3⅜" x 1".

Cut 11" x 8½" cardstock to 8½" x 5½". Score and fold to form a card.

Layer and adhere cardstock pieces and quote trim to front of card as shown in photograph, or as desired.

Grass: Use decorative-edged scissors to cut grass from one long edge of light green cardstock. Adhere grass to card.

Sidewalk: Using Sidewalk Template, trace and cut out sidewalk from gray cardstock. Adhere sidewalk to grass 1" from right edge, keeping bottom edges of cardstock even as shown.

Picket fence: Cut two 2¼" and two 1" white strips for rails. Adhere strips horizontally to grass. Cut thirteen ¾" white strips. Cut a point at one end of each strip for pickets. Adhere pickets over rails, beginning ⅛" away from sides, and ⅛" apart.

House: Using House Template, trace and cut out house from yellow cardstock. Center house with sidewalk, and adhere to front of

Welcome to
Your New Home

Suggestion:

Try making the house with quilling paper and cardstock colors that match the outside of your new home or the recipient's new home.

card. *Notes: Bottom edge of house should be even with top of sidewalk. House will overlap top deckled edge of grass about 1/8".*

Roof: Cut two 1⁵/₈" black strips from quilling paper. Adhere to roof of house, overlapping strips at top point.

Adhere all quilled shapes to card as shown, or as desired.

Actual size

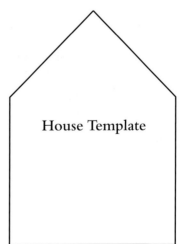

House Template

Sidewalk Template

Get Well Card

Finished Size: $4\frac{1}{4}$" x $5\frac{1}{2}$"

Quilling Materials:

Note: Refer to Quilling Tools and Supplies on pages 12–15.

• $\frac{1}{8}$"-wide quilling papers:

Blue parchment
White/silver gilded edge

Quilling Instructions:

Note: Refer to Quilling Techniques on pages 18–25.

Clouds: Quill one 18" and two 15" blue loose circles. Pinch into cloud shapes as desired.

Lightning bolt: Cut 2" white/silver strip. Fold back and forth at $\frac{1}{2}$", $\frac{3}{4}$", $1\frac{1}{4}$", and $1\frac{1}{2}$" to form lightning bolt.

Raindrops: Cut 12" white/silver gilded edge quilling paper in half lengthwise to $\frac{1}{16}$"-wide. Cut into eight $1\frac{1}{2}$" strips and use half with gilded edge to quill teardrops.

Card Materials:

• Cardstocks:

Medium blue: $5\frac{1}{4}$" x 4", $3\frac{1}{4}$" x $1\frac{1}{2}$", $2\frac{3}{4}$" x 2"
White: 11" x $8\frac{1}{2}$"

• Paper:

Blue parchment: 5" x $3\frac{3}{4}$"

• Computer/color printer or marker

• Corner edgers

• Corner rounder

• Marker: pale blue

Card Instructions:

Print "Feeling under the weather?" and "Hope you get well soon" on 11" x $8\frac{1}{2}$" cardstock. *Note: If computer and printer are not available, hand-print words with marker.*

Trim down and detail with corner edgers. Draw dashed lines close to edges with marker.

Use corner edgers on other cardstock pieces. Layer and adhere together as shown in photograph.

Cut remaining 11" x $8\frac{1}{2}$" cardstock to $8\frac{1}{2}$" x $5\frac{1}{2}$"; score and fold to form card.

Round corners of card, desired cardstock, and paper. Layer and adhere cardstock, paper, sentiment pieces, and quilled shapes to card as shown, or as desired.

Sympathy Card

Finished Size: 5½" x 4¼"

Quilling Materials:

Note: Refer to Quilling Tools and Supplies on pages 12–15.

- ⅛"-wide quilling papers:
  Burgundy
  Garnet

Quilling Instructions:

Note: Refer to Quilling Techniques on pages 18–25.

Quill eight 3" burgundy teardrops.

Quill sixteen 2" garnet teardrops.

Card Materials:

- Cardstocks:

  Burgundy: 5¼" x 4", 3¾" x 2¾"

  Pink: 5" x 3¾"

  White: 8½" x 5½", 3½" x 2½"

- Ink pad: burgundy

- Rubber stamp: "With Sympathy"

- Scratch paper

Card Instructions:

Score and fold 8½" x 5½" cardstock to form card.

Rubber-stamp sentiment onto cardstock.

Trace Oval Template onto scratch paper, including placement marks. Cut out.

Center and trace cut-out oval over stamped words on cardstock. Cut out.

Center word cutout on 3¾" x 2¾" burgundy cardstock and cut out, leaving a 1/16" border.

Center and adhere all cardstock to front of card as shown in photograph, or as desired. Using placement marks on template, adhere quilled shapes to front of card.

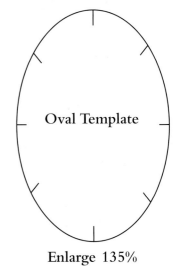

Oval Template

Enlarge 135%

Valentine Card

Finished Size: 4¼" x 5½"

Quilling Materials:

Note: Refer to Quilling Tools and Supplies on pages 12–15.

- ⅛"-wide quilling papers:

    Pink

    True red

Quilling Instructions:

Note: Refer to Quilling Techniques on pages 18–25.

Quill one 4" pink heart.

Quill two 3" red hearts.

Card Materials:

- Cardstocks:

    Dark pink: 1⅛"-square, (2) 1"-square

    Light pink: 1¼"-square, (2) 1⅛"-square

    White: 8½" x 5½", 1"-square, (2) ⅞"-square

- Paper:

    Red/pink patterned: (2) 5⅜" x 2"

Card Instructions:

Score 2⅛" in on both ends of 8½" x 5½" cardstock. Fold on scored lines to meet in middle, forming front flaps.

Center and adhere patterned paper to left- and right-front flaps of card.

Layer and adhere cardstock squares together as shown in photograph, or as desired. Adhere layered squares diagonally to left-front flap of card only.

Adhere hearts to squares as shown, or as desired.

St. Patrick's Day Card

Finished Size: 4¼" x 5½"

Quilling Materials:

Note: Refer to Quilling Tools and Supplies on pages 12–15.

- ⅛"-wide quilling paper: Holiday green

Quilling Instructions:

Note: Refer to Quilling Techniques on pages 18–25.

Clovers (make 4): Quill four 2" green hearts. Adhere hearts together with points meeting in center.

Cut ¾" green strip. Curve strip with fingers and adhere end between two hearts to form stem. Trim stem as needed.

Card Materials:

- Cardstocks:
    Dark green: 5¼" x 4"
    Light green: 5¼" x 4", 6" x 1½"
    White: 8½" x 5½"
- Paper:
    White/green patterned: 4"-square
- Corner rounder
- Scratch paper

Card Instructions:

Score and fold 8½" x 5½" cardstock to form card.

Round corners of card and 5¼" x 4" light green cardstock. Center and adhere together.

Trace three Clover Templates onto scratch paper and cut out. Trace Large Clover Template onto 5¼" x 4" dark green cardstock and Medium Clover Template onto paper. Cut out.

Center and adhere clovers to card.

Trace four small clovers onto 6" x 1½" cardstock and cut out. Arrange and adhere to front of card as shown in photograph, or as desired.

Adhere one quilled clover to each small clover.

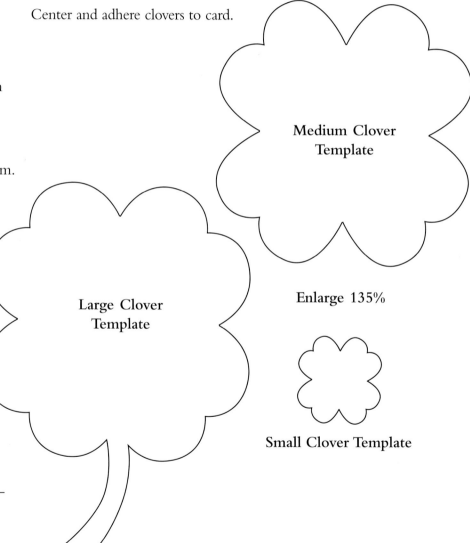

Medium Clover Template

Enlarge 135%

Large Clover Template

Small Clover Template

Easter Cross Card

Finished Size: 5" x 6½"

Quilling Materials:

Note: Refer to Quilling Tools and Supplies on pages 12–15.

- ⅛"-wide quilling paper:
    White/gold gilded edge
- Scratch paper
- Waxed paper

Quilling Instructions:

Note: Refer to Quilling Techniques on pages 18–25.

Draw intersecting perpendicular lines on scratch paper. Place underneath waxed paper on quilling designer board to use as a template for cross construction.

Quill 3" loose circle and pin to intersection of perpendicular lines on template. Make sure gilded edge of paper faces up.

Cut one 2½" strip and three 1½" strips for lines of cross. Adhere one end of each strip to loose circle so that strips run over template lines.

Quill twenty 2½" S-scrolls to about ½" in length. *Note: Quill half the strips to form a traditional "S" shape, and the other half backward, in order to achieve the mirror-image effect.* (See Fig. 2A)

Adhere S-scrolls to lines of cross in mirror-image pattern on each side of cross lines.

Begin at center cross and work outward to end of lines, adhering four S-scrolls on shorter arms, and eight S-scrolls on long arm. Trim any excess paper from between last S-scrolls on each arm. (See Fig. 2B)

Quill four 2" teardrops. Adhere pointed end of teardrops to outer end of each cross line between last S-scrolls of each line.

Quill four 2½" open hearts. *Note: Do not adhere rolls of hearts together in middle.* Adhere hearts to inside corners of cross between lines. (See Fig. 2C)

Quill eight 2½" mirror-image S-scrolls.

Card Materials:

- Cardstocks:
    Lavender: 6¼" x 4¾"
    Light gray: 11" x 8½"
    Purple: 4½" x 3½",
    3½" x 1¼"
    White: 10" x 6½"
- Computer/color printer or marker
- Corner edgers
- Corner rounder

Card Instructions:

Score and fold 10" x 6½" cardstock to form card.

Round corners of card and 6¼" x 4¾" cardstock. Center and adhere cardstock to card.

Fig. 2A

Fig. 2B

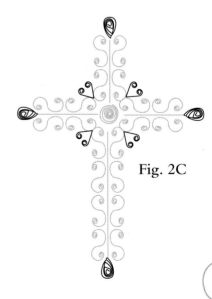

Fig. 2C

Suggestion:

Attach a hanging loop made with thread or embroidery floss to the top of the quilled cross, then lightly tack cross to front of card for a removable gift.

Print "He Is Risen" on 11" x 8¹/₂" cardstock. *Note: If computer and printer are not available, hand-print words with marker.* Evenly trim to 3¹/₄" x 1". Cut 4¹/₄" x 3¹/₄" piece from remainder of cardstock.

Use corner edgers on cardstock pieces. *Note: Corner edgers are used in one direction on larger cardstock pieces and in the other direction on smaller cardstock pieces.* Layer and adhere to card as shown, in photograph, or as desired.

Center and adhere cross and S-scrolls to front of card as shown in photograph, or as desired.

Easter Egg Card

Finished Size: 4¼" x 5½"

Quilling Materials:

Note: Refer to Quilling Tools and Supplies on pages 12–15.

- ⅛"-wide quilling papers:
    Bright white
    Magenta
    Meadow green
    Periwinkle
    Purple
    Yellow

Quilling Instructions:

Note: Refer to Quilling Techniques on pages 18–25.

Quill the following shapes from 2" strips:

    Seven magenta loose circles
    Seven purple marquises
    Five yellow S-scrolls
    Seven green marquises
    Seven periwinkle loose circles
    One periwinkle S-scroll
    One white S-scroll

Card Materials:

- Cardstocks:

    Lavender: 3¾" x 5"
    White: 8½" x 5½", 2½" x 2", 1¾" x ⅜"

- Paper:

    Purple: 4" x 5¼", 1½"-square

- 10" x ¼"-wide white organdy ribbon

- Scratch paper

Card Instructions:

Score and fold 8½" x 5½" cardstock to form card.

Trace Pot Template and Egg Template onto scratch paper, then cut out. Trace pot onto 1½"-square paper and egg onto 2½" x 2" cardstock. Cut shapes out.

Layer and adhere cardstock pieces, pot, egg, and 1½" purple strip for stem to card as shown in photograph, or as desired.

Arrange and adhere quilled shapes as shown, or as desired.

Tie a bow in ribbon. Trim ends and adhere to top of stem just below egg.

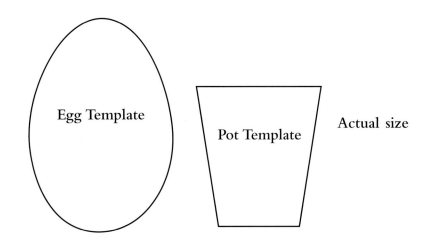

Egg Template

Pot Template

Actual size

Mother's Day Card

Finished Size: 5" x 6$\frac{1}{2}$"

Quilling Materials:

Note: Refer to Quilling Tools and Supplies on pages 12–15.

- $\frac{1}{8}$"-wide quilling paper:

    Lilac

- $\frac{1}{16}$"-wide quilling papers:

    Lilac

    Maize

    Pale green

    Pale peach

    Pink

    Sky blue

Quilling Instructions:

Note: Refer to Quilling Techniques on pages 18–25.

Daisy (make 2): Quill six 3" pink teardrops. Adhere together with points in center.

Quill 2" maize grape roll. Adhere on top of center.

Daffodil: Quill five 3" peach marquises. Adhere together with points in center.

Quill 2" maize grape roll of contrasting color. Adhere on top of center.

Half daffodil: Quill three 3" peach marquises. Adhere together with points in center to form half flower.

Quill 2" maize grape roll. Adhere next to center.

Large forget-me-not: Quill four 3" blue bunny ears. Adhere together with curved edges in center.

Quill 2" maize grape roll. Adhere on top of center.

Small forget-me-not (make 2): Quill four 2$\frac{1}{2}$" maize bunny ears. Adhere together with curved edges in center.

Quill 2" peach grape roll of contrasting color. Adhere on top of center.

Lilacs (make 2): Quill five 2" lilac bunny ears from $\frac{1}{16}$"-wide paper. Adhere curved edge of one bunny ear to end of 4" green strip. Arrange and adhere two bunny ears on each side of strip as shown in photograph.

Leaf (make 17): Quill 2" green marquise.

Bow: Cut 3" strip $\frac{1}{8}$"-wide lilac. Adhere both ends to center of strip to form loops.

Wrap $\frac{1}{2}$" strip vertically around center and adhere. Trim excess.

Cut two 1$\frac{1}{4}$" strips for tails. Cut notch in one end of each strip.

Overlap and adhere other ends in a V-shape. Adhere overlap to center back of loops.

Card Materials:

- Cardstock:

    White: 11" x 8$\frac{1}{2}$", 10" x 6$\frac{1}{2}$"

- Papers:

    Lavender: 6$\frac{1}{4}$" x 4$\frac{3}{4}$"
    Pink: 4" x 5"

- Computer/color printer or marker

- Corner rounder

- Decorative-edged scissors: mini-scallop

- Marker: lavender

- Scratch paper

Card Instructions:

Score and fold 10" x 6$\frac{1}{2}$" cardstock to form card. Round corners of card and 6$\frac{1}{4}$" x 4$\frac{3}{4}$" paper. Adhere paper to card.

Print "Happy Mother's Day" on 11" x 8$\frac{1}{2}$" cardstock. *Note: If computer and printer are not available, hand-print words with marker.*

Trim wording piece to 4$\frac{1}{2}$" x 6", round corners, and adhere to card as shown in photograph, or as desired.

Trace Oval Template onto scratch paper and cut out. Trace oval cutout onto remainder of cardstock used to print wording, and cut out. Center and adhere to 4" x 5" paper.

Oval Template

Enlarge 200%

With decorative-edged scissors, cut paper around oval shape, leaving $1/8$" border. Center and adhere to front of card.

Make dashed lines around edges of $4^1/2$" x 6" cardstock piece with marker.

Arrange and adhere quilled flowers on oval as shown, or as desired.

Cut seven flower stems from green quilling paper, ranging in length from $2^1/2$" to 4". Curve as needed. Arrange and adhere stems, trimming bottoms as needed.

Arrange and adhere leaves next to stems. Center and adhere bow on top of stems as shown.

Father's Day Card

Finished Size: 6½" x 5"

Quilling Materials:

Note: Refer to Quilling Tools and Supplies on pages 12–15.

- ⅛"-wide quilling papers:
    - Bright white
    - Cadet blue
    - Celestial blue sparkling
    - Gold
    - Tan
    - White/silver gilded edge
    - Yellow
- 1/16"-wide quilling paper:
    - Bright White
- Cardstocks:
    - Black: ½"-square, 2"x ½"
    - Blue: ⅜" x ½"
    - Green: 1"-square
- Papers:
    - Dark shiny silver: 2" x ½"
    - Shiny silver: 2½" x ½"
- ⅝"-diameter circle punch
- Round toothpick
- Sewing needle
- Sewing thread: gray

Quilling Instructions:

Note: Refer to Quilling Techniques on pages 18–25.

Football:
Quill 9" gold marquise.

Cut two ⅜" strips of 1/16"-wide white quilling paper. Adhere on top of football, ⅛" away from ends. Trim excess.

Adhere two 3/16" lengths of 1/16"-wide white quilling strips evenly spaced across one 5/16" length of 1/16"-wide strip for stitching. Adhere to top of football as shown in photograph.

Bat: Quill 3/16" x 1¼" rectangle from 23" tan strip, using largest hole on quilling designer board. Pinch a slight indentation into long sides of rectangle ¼" from one end.

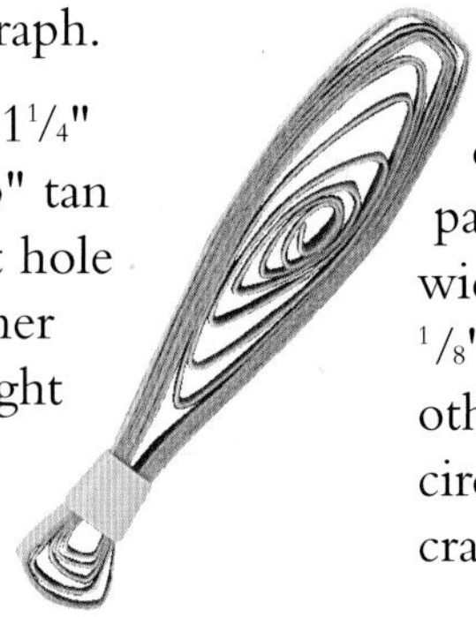

Adhere ⅝" tan strip around indentation ⅛" away from end to form neck of bat. Trim excess.

Baseball: Quill 2" white loose circle.

Fishing pole: Taper 2½" x ½" silver paper down to ¼" at one end. Roll 2½" edge of paper around toothpick. Remove toothpick. Adjust roll with fingers so roll is narrower at tapered end to form pole. Adhere edges.

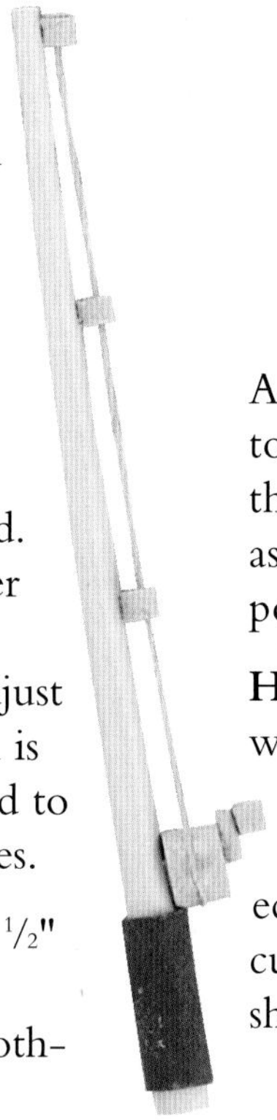

Roll ⅜" edge of ⅜" x ½" blue cardstock around toothpick. Remove tooth-

pick. Adhere roll around pole 1/16" away from wider end for handle.

Quill 4" celestial blue tight circle for reel.

Cut two ½" celestial blue strips in half lengthwise, and use to quill one ½" tight circle and three ½" loose circles on needle tool. Set loose circles aside.

Quill ¼" celestial blue tight circle with ⅛"-wide quilling paper. Adhere bottom of 1/16"-wide tight circle to end of side of ⅛"-wide tight circle. Adhere other end of same ⅛"-wide tight circle to center of reel to form crank as shown. (See Fig. 3A)

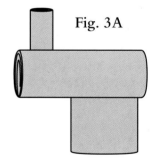

Fig. 3A

Adhere reel to side of pole next to handle as shown. Adhere three loose circles that were set aside, evenly spaced to side of pole as shown.

Hook: Cut ½" strip of ⅛"-wide white/silver paper lengthwise in half to be 1/16"-wide, making sure to use half with gilded edge. Cut a point at one end and curve pointed end into hook shape with fingers.

Thread needle with 9" thread. Carefully pierce hole in straight end of hook with needle and push needle through hole. Tie square knot in end of thread next to hook. Place drop of adhesive on knot and cut off short end of thread next to knot.

Pass needle and thread through center hole of three loose circles, starting at end of pole without handle. Remove thread from needle. With $1\frac{1}{4}$" of thread between tip of pole and top of hook, adhere free end of thread around reel once and trim excess.

Fish: Quill 6" white/silver eccentric loose circle. Place in 6" hole on quilling designer board, with gilded edge face down. Remove circle and squeeze into oval shape with adhered rolls at one end, forming head with eye and body.

Quill 2" white/silver triangle for tail. Quill two 1" white/silver triangles with one $\frac{1}{8}$" side and two $\frac{3}{16}$" sides for fins.

Adhere shapes together to form fish as shown.

Golf club: Quill 3" dark blue triangle with one $\frac{1}{4}$" side and two slightly rounded $\frac{3}{8}$" sides to form head of club.

Roll 2" edge of 2" x $\frac{1}{2}$" dark silver paper tightly and smoothly around toothpick to form shaft. Adhere edges together, remove toothpick.

Roll ½"-square black cardstock around toothpick. Remove toothpick. Adhere around end of shaft. Adhere head of club to other end of shaft as shown.

Golf ball: Quill 2" loose circle on needle tool from ⅛"-wide white quilling paper.

Quill 1" tan triangle with one ¹⁄₁₆" side and two ⅛" sides. Squeeze ⅛" sides to form tee. Adhere ¹⁄₁₆" side of tee to edge of circle.

Golf flag/pole/putting green: Roll 2" edge of 2" x ½" black cardstock tightly and smoothly around toothpick to form pole. Adhere edges together; remove toothpick.

Quill 6" yellow triangle with one ⁵⁄₁₆" side and two ⁹⁄₁₆" sides for flag. Punch green circle from 1"-square cardstock for putting green.

Adhere bottom end of pole to center of circle as shown. Adhere short side of flag to left edge of top end of pole.

Tie: Quill 9" cadet blue teardrop.

Pinch ⅛" away on each side of teardrop point. Pinch other end to form flat ⅛" end. Pinch ⅛" away from each side of flattened end.

Squeeze indentation next to four points on flattened end and adhere ½" strip around indentation.

Card Materials:

- Cardstocks:

    Blue: 6¼" x 4¾", 3¾" x 2¼"
    White: 11" x 8½", 10" x 6½"

- Paper:

    Blue plaid: 6" x 4½"

- Computer/color printer or marker

- Marker: blue

Card Instructions:

Score and fold 10" x 6½" cardstock to form card.

Center and adhere 6¼" x 4¾" cardstock and 6" x 4½" paper to front of card.

Print "Happy Father's Day" on 11" x 8½" cardstock. *Note: If computer and printer are not available, hand-print words with marker.*

Evenly trim to 3½" x 2". Draw dashed lines close to edges.

Center and adhere to 3¾" x 2¼" cardstock. Center and adhere to front of card.

Arrange and adhere quilled shapes to front of card as shown in photograph on page 59, or as desired.

Shalom Card

Finished Size: 4¼" x 5½"

Quilling Materials:

Note: Refer to Quilling Tools and Supplies on pages 12–15.

- ⅛"-wide quilling papers:

    Midnight blue sparkling
    Starlight silver sparkling

Quilling Instructions:

Note: Refer to Quilling Techniques on pages 18–25.

Star of David: Quill twelve 6" silver triangles. Adhere six together to form hexagon.

Wrap and adhere midnight blue quilling paper two times around each remaining triangle. Adhere one wrapped triangle to each side of hexagon to form Star of David.

Card Materials:

- Cardstocks:

    Medium blue: 2¼" x 2"
    White: 8½" x 5½",
    2¾" x 1¼"

- Papers:

    Blue patterned: 5¼" x 4"
    Dark blue shiny: 2⅝" x 2⅜"
    Yellow/gold: 2⅞" x 2⅝"

- Corner rounder

- Marker: blue

Card Instructions:

Score and fold 8½" x 5½" cardstock to form card.

Round corners of card, papers, and all cardstock.

Adhere cardstock and paper to front of card as shown in photograph, or as desired.

Write "Shalom" in ½"-tall letters centered on cardstock with marker. Draw dashed lines close to edges.

Center and adhere Star of David to card as shown.

Independence Day Card

Finished Size: 5" x 6½"

Quilling Materials:

Note: Refer to Quilling Tools and Supplies on pages 12–15.

- ⅛"-wide quilling papers:

  Bright white
  True red
  Twighlight gold sparkling
  Violet

Quilling Instructions:

Note: Refer to Quilling Techniques on pages 18–25.

Flag: Quill three 3" violet S-scrolls, five 3" white S-scrolls, and seven 3" red S-scrolls. Adhere together in rows, then adhere rows together as shown in photograph.

Quill four 1" white tight circles for stars. Adhere stars between S-scrolls in blue (violet) flag section as shown.

Flagpole: Quill 1½" gold loose circle on needle tool.

Cut two 2" gold strips. Adhere together to make a stronger strip for flagpole.

Adhere flagpole to left edge of flag. Adhere loose circle to top of flagpole.

Card Materials:

- Cardstocks:

  Dark blue: 3¼" x 2", 1½" x ¾"
  Gold: 6¼" x 4¾"
  Red: 2¾"-square, 1½" x ¾"
  White: 10" x 6½", 6" x 4½", 3" x 1¾", 2½"-square
  Yellow/gold: 2¼" x ¾"

- ⅛"-diameter circle punch

- ½" star punch

- Ink pad: blue

- Marker: black

- Rubber stamp: "God Bless America"

Card Instructions:

Score and fold 10" x 6½" cardstock to form card.

Center and adhere gold cardstock and 4½" x 6" white cardstock to front of card.

With ruler and pencil, measure and mark lightly ⅛" from edges of layered white cardstock: five marks (counting corners) evenly spaced across 4½" sides and seven marks (counting corners) evenly spaced across 6" sides.

With marker, draw small stars on corner marks and every other mark along each side. Draw small circles on remaining marks between stars.

With ruler and marker, draw three lines between each star and circle ⅛" away from edges of cardstock. Erase pencil marks.

With ink pad and rubber stamp, stamp "God Bless America" in center of 3" x 1¾" white cardstock.

With ruler and pencil, measure and mark lightly ⅛" from edges of 3" x 1¾" white cardstock: five marks (counting corners) evenly spaced across 3" sides and three marks (counting corners) evenly spaced across 1¾" sides.

With ruler and pencil, measure and mark lightly ⅛" from edges of 2½"-square white cardstock: five marks (counting corners) evenly spaced across each side.

Punch two stars and fourteen circles from both 1½" x ¾" red cardstock and 1½" x ¾" dark blue cardstock. Punch three stars from yellow/gold cardstock.

Adhere red and blue punched circles to marks on both marked pieces of white cardstock as shown in photograph. With ruler and marker, draw lines between circles ⅛" away from edges of cardstock.

Layer and adhere 3" x 1¾" white cardstock to 3¼" x 2" dark blue cardstock, and 2½"-square white cardstock to 2¾"-square red cardstock.

Suggestion:

Use this technique to create cards celebrating Cinco de Mayo, or Independence Day celebrations of other nations.

Adhere assembled flag to center of 2½"-square white cardstock.

Arrange and adhere "God Bless America," quilled flag, and stars to front of card as shown, or as desired.

Halloween Card

Finished Size: 6½" x 5"

Quilling Materials:

Note: Refer to Quilling Tools and Supplies on pages 12–15.

- ⅛"-wide quilling papers:

    Black
    Bright white
    Bright yellow
    Holiday green
    Orange

Quilling Instructions:

Note: Refer to Quilling Techniques on pages 18–25.

Candy corn (make 7): Quill 2" white triangle with one ³/₁₆" side and two ¼" slightly rounded sides.

Quill 3" yellow loose circle. Pinch and shape into a trapezoid with ³/₁₆" top, ¼" sides, and ⁵/₁₆" base.

Quill 4" orange loose circle. Pinch and shape into a trapezoid with ⁵/₁₆" top, ³/₁₆" sides, and ⅜" base. Adhere three shapes together as shown in photograph. Pin together until adhesive dries.

Pumpkin (make 7): Quill 6" orange loose circle. Push joined end toward center of circle to form pumpkin.

Quill 1½" green triangle with one ⅛" side and two ³/₁₆" sides. Curve one long side slightly to form stem.

Adhere ⅛" side of stem to indented end of pumpkin. Pin together until adhesive dries.

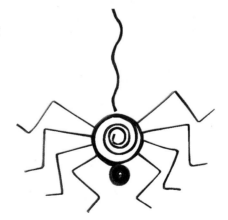

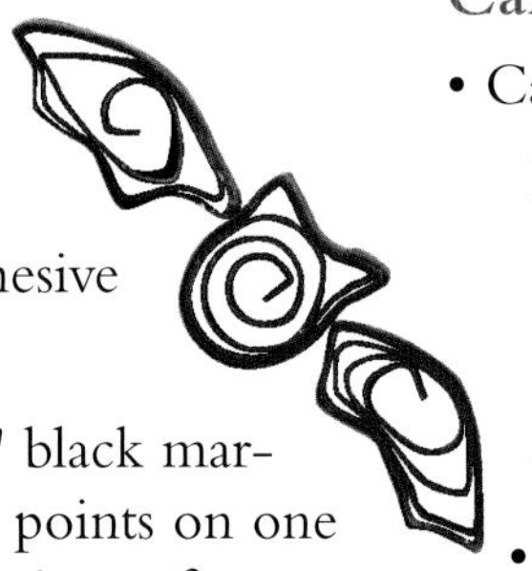

Bat: Quill two 4" black marquises. Pinch two points on one side of each marquise to form wings.

Quill 4" black loose circle. Pinch two ears about ¼" apart to form head. Adhere wings to sides of head.

Spider: Quill 4" black loose circle for body and 2" black tight circle for head. Adhere head to body.

Cut eight ¾" black strips for legs. Fold each strip in half. Fold back ⅛" on one end of each strip for foot. On other end of strips, trim off ³/₁₆" on two strips, ⅛" on two strips, and ¹/₁₆" on four strips.

Card Materials:

- Cardstocks:

    Black: 3¾" x 2⅜",
    (14) ¹⁵/₁₆" x ⅞"
    Deep yellow: (7) 1³/₁₆" x 1⅛"
    Orange: (7) 1³/₁₆" x 1⅛"
    White: 11" x 8½", 10" x 6½"

- Computer/color printer or marker

- Marker: black

Card Instructions:

Score and fold 10" x 6½" cardstock to form card.

Center and adhere 3¾" x 2⅜" black cardstock to front of card.

Arrange and adhere orange and yellow cardstock pieces around black center on front of card, then adhere black pieces layered askew as shown in photograph.

Print "TRICK OR TREAT" on 11" x 8½" cardstock. *Note: If computer and printer are not available, hand-print words with marker.*

Evenly trim to 3½" x 2⅛". Center and adhere to front of card.

Arrange and adhere spider parts with longest legs on top, candy corn, bat, and pumpkins to front of card as shown, or as desired. Draw wavy string above spider with marker.

Thanksgiving Card

Finished Size: 5¹/₂" x 4¹/₄"

Quilling Materials:

Note: Refer to Quilling Tools and Supplies on pages 12–15.

- ¹/₈"-wide quilling papers:

    Forest green

    Robin brown
- ¹/₁₆"-wide quilling papers:

    Beech brown

    Fawn

Quilling Instructions:

Note: Refer to Quilling Techniques on pages 18–25.

Pumpkin: Quill 7¹/₂" robin brown loose circle. Push joined end toward center of circle to form pumpkin.

Quill 2" green teardrop. Pinch again ¹/₈" away from first point and curve slightly to one side to form stem. Adhere curved end of stem to pushed in end of pumpkin. Pin together until adhesive dries.

Roll ¹/₄" on one end of 1" beech brown strip with needle tool.

Make a spiral with the remainder of the strip. Repeat with another 1" beech brown strip, making sure to reverse direction of spiral on second strip. Adhere flat end of spiral sections behind top of pumpkin and shape spirals with fingers as desired.

Wheat spray (make 2): Slightly curve 1⁵/₈" fawn strip.

Quill six 1¹/₂", four 1¹/₄", and two 1" fawn teardrops. Arrange and adhere curved end of teardrops to both sides of 1⁵/₈" fawn strip, starting ¹/₂" from one end of strip. Start with two smallest teardrops and end with six largest teardrops.

Adhere three ³/₈" slightly curved fawn strips to each side of 1⁵/₈" fawn strip, starting at base of smallest teardrops as shown in photograph. Trim as desired.

Scroll (make 2): Fold 1³/₄" beech brown strip at ³/₄". Roll ³/₈" on each end outward with needle tool. Adhere fold together and curve strip toward shorter side as shown.

Card Materials:

- Cardstocks:

    Gold: 4¹/₂" x 3¹/₄"

    Ivory: 8¹/₂" x 5¹/₂", 4¹/₄" x 3"
- Paper:

    Brown plaid: 5¹/₄" x 4"
- Corner rounder
- Marker: brown

Card Instructions:

Score and fold 8¹/₂" x 5¹/₂" cardstock and adhere together to form card. Center and adhere paper to front of card.

Round corners of 4¹/₂" x 3¹/₄" cardstock and 4¹/₄" x 3" cardstock. Write "Happy Thanksgiving" on cardstock with marker as shown in photograph, or as desired. Draw dashed lines around edges. Layer and adhere cardstock pieces to front of card.

Center and adhere quilled pumpkin, wheat sprays, and scrolls on card as shown, or as desired.

Suggestion:

Use any shade of green and your choice of three shades brown quilling paper.

Hanukkah Card

Finished Size: 5" x 6$\frac{1}{2}$"

Quilling Materials:

Note: Refer to Quilling Tools and Supplies on pages 12–15.

- $\frac{1}{8}$"-wide quilling papers:

   Celestial blue sparkling
   Midnight blue sparkling
   Twilight gold sparkling

Quilling Instructions:

Note: Refer to Quilling Techniques on pages 18–25.

Menorah stand: Quill three 12" midnight blue triangles with one 1" side and two $\frac{5}{8}$" sides. Adhere $\frac{5}{8}$" sides of triangles together in a row with 1" side of center triangle on the bottom and 1" side of two other triangles on the top.

Quill 6" midnight blue rectangle with two $\frac{1}{8}$" sides and two $\frac{9}{16}$" sides.

Quill 6" midnight blue half circle with $\frac{1}{2}$" base. Center and adhere one $\frac{1}{8}$" side of rectangle to bottom of center triangle and other $\frac{1}{8}$" side of rectangle to rounded part of half circle.

Candles: Quill 9" celestial blue rectangle with two $\frac{1}{8}$" sides and two $\frac{7}{8}$" sides.

Quill eight 6" celestial blue rectangles with two $\frac{1}{8}$" sides and two $\frac{5}{8}$" sides. Adhere one $\frac{1}{8}$" side of candles evenly spaced across top of stand with tallest candle in center.

Flames: Quill one 2$\frac{1}{2}$" gold teardrop and eight 1$\frac{1}{2}$" gold teardrops on needle tool. Adhere rounded end of each teardrop to top of each candle with 2$\frac{1}{2}$" teardrop adhered to center candle.

Card Materials:

- Cardstocks:

   Blue/gray: 6" x 4$\frac{1}{2}$"
   White: 10" x 6$\frac{1}{2}$", 3" x 2$\frac{3}{4}$", 2$\frac{3}{4}$" x 1$\frac{3}{4}$"

- Paper:

   Shiny dark blue: 6$\frac{1}{4}$" x 4$\frac{3}{4}$", 3$\frac{1}{4}$" x 3", 3" x 2"

- Corner edgers

- Corner rounder

- Marker: gray

Card Instructions:

Score and fold 10" x 6$\frac{1}{2}$" white cardstock to form card.

Round corners of card, 6$\frac{1}{4}$" x 4$\frac{3}{4}$" shiny dark blue paper, and blue/gray cardstock. Center and adhere dark blue paper and blue/gray cardstock to front of card.

Use corner edgers on remaining white cardstock and dark blue paper. Draw dashed lines close to edges on both pieces of white cardstock. Layer and adhere cardstock and paper pieces to front of card as shown in photograph, or as desired.

Write "Happy Hanukkah" on 2$\frac{3}{4}$" x 1$\frac{3}{4}$" white cardstock with marker. Center and adhere assembled menorah to card as shown, or as desired.

Christmas Card

Finished Size: 4¼" x 5½"

Quilling Materials:

Note: Refer to Quilling Tools and Supplies on pages 12–15.

- ⅛"-wide quilling papers:

    Holiday green
    True red

- ¼"-wide quilling paper:

    Bright white

- Scratch paper
- Waxed paper

Quilling Instructions:

Note: Refer to Quilling Techniques on pages 18–25.

Wreath: Quill twelve 3" green teardrops and twelve 2" green C-scrolls.

Quill five 2" red tight circles.

Trace Circle Template onto scratch paper. Cover template with waxed paper to keep shapes from sticking.

Arrange and adhere teardrops together around circle template, points facing outward. Adhere curved edge of C-scrolls between teardrop points. Adhere tight circles to inside curve of every other C-scroll. *Note: There will be a space of three C-scrolls without a tight circle. This will be the top of the wreath where the bow will be adhered.*

Bow loops: Loop and adhere ends of 3" length of white quilling paper to back center of loop. Wrap and adhere 3" red strip around white loop.

Center and vertically adhere one end of 1" white strip to back center of loop. Wrap and adhere around. Wrap and adhere 1" red strip over vertically adhered white strip. Trim excess. *Note: Be sure to adhere red and white strips around bow loops one at a time, or they will look bunched up once dried.*

Bow tails: Center and adhere two 1¼" red strips to two 1¼" white strips. Cut notch in bottom of each strip. Cut tops of strips at a slight angle in opposite directions.

Overlap and adhere at angled ends; adhere to back center of loop.

Card Materials:

- Cardstock:

    White: 8½" x 5½",
    2½" x 2¼", 2¼" x ¾"

- Papers:

    Green: 5¼" x 4"
    Green striped: 5" x 3¾"
    Red: 2¾" x 2½", 2½" x 1"

- Corner edgers
- Corner rounder
- Marker: red

Card Instructions:

Score and fold 8½" x 5½" cardstock to form card.

Round corners of card, green paper, and green striped paper. Layer and adhere together.

Use corner edgers on two remaining pieces of white cardstock and on both pieces of red paper. Draw dashed lines close to edges on both pieces of white cardstock with marker.

Write "NOEL" on 2¼" x ¾" white cardstock with marker. Center and adhere white cardstock pieces to red papers. Position and adhere on front of card as shown in photograph, or as desired.

Adhere bow to space at top of wreath. Center and adhere wreath to front of card.

Actual size

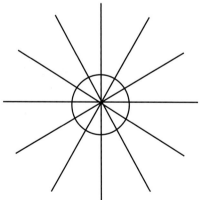

Circle Template

71

Suggestion:

Attach a hanging loop made from thread or embroidery floss to top of quilled wreath, then lightly tack wreath to front of card for a removable ornament.

To Love
and
To Cherish

3

Quilled Scrapbook Pages

Quilling page protectors are strongly suggested to prevent quilling from being damaged. Since the page protectors do not accommodate traditional 12"-square pages, simply trim background cardstock, paper, border strips, etc., $\frac{1}{8}$" before assembly, so finished size is $11\frac{7}{8}$" square. Resources are listed in the back of this book if page protectors are not available in your local craft store.

Due to personal color preference, desire to coordinate color with photographs, or a lack of supplies, you may want to change the colors of cardstock, paper, quilling papers, or other supplies used. If you have a great photograph in which the subject is smaller than you'd like it to be, enlarge it on a scanner or color copier to fit the scrapbook page.

Although not all of the pages in this book have a space for journaling, one can be added to any of the projects.

Wedding Page

Finished Size: 12" square

Quilling Materials:

Note: Refer to Quilling Tools and Supplies on pages 12–15.

- $1/16$"-wide quilling papers:

  Bright white

  Pink
- $1/8$"-wide quilling paper:

  Bright white
- Cardstock:

  White

Quilling Instructions:

Note: Refer to Quilling Techniques on pages 18–25.

Tiered cake: Using ruler and pencil, make four evenly spaced marks near one $1^1/2$" edge on back of $1^1/2$" x $^{11}/_{16}$" cardstock, making first and last marks $1/8$" away from $^{11}/_{16}$" sides.

Using $1/16$"-wide quilling papers, adhere four white 1" strips across marks, perpendicular to and overlapping long edge of cardstock $3/8$". (See Fig. 4A)

Adhere remaining ends of strips $3/8$" onto 2" x $3/4$" cardstock, $1/4$" above $1^1/2$" x $^{11}/_{16}$" cardstock. (See Fig. 4B) Repeat with 1" x $5/8$" cardstock, using three 1" strips to create tiers. (See Fig. 4C)

Quilled cake decorations: Quill twenty-two 1" open hearts, seventeen $1^1/2$" S-scrolls, twelve $1^1/2$" loose circles, and three $1^1/2$" hearts with $1/16$"-wide white strips. Arrange and adhere quilled shapes to cake as shown in photograph, or as desired.

Goblet (make 2 with $1/8$"-wide quilling papers): Quill 6" white half circle with $5/16$" base. Squeeze curved part slightly to form top of goblet.

Quill 2" white marquise. Flatten for stem.

Quill 2" white uneven marquise with one $5/16$" side for base. Adhere three pieces together to form goblet.

Hearts: Quill two 1" pink hearts.

Page Materials:

- Cardstocks:

  Dark pink

  Lavender

  Pink

  Purple

  White
- Decorative-edged scissors: mini-scallop
- Marker: purple
- Rubber stamp: "To Love and To Cherish"

Page Instructions:

Trim three wedding photos as needed.

Ink rubber stamp with marker. Huff on stamp to moisten ink. Center and stamp on 3" x 2" white cardstock.

Trim edges of desired cardstock pieces with mini-scallop scissors.

Layer and adhere cardstock pieces and photos to page as shown in photograph, or as desired.

Adhere quilled cake and goblets to page as shown, or as desired.

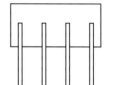

Fig. 4A

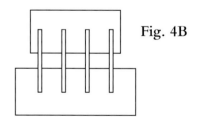

Fig. 4B

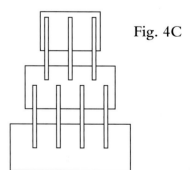

Fig. 4C

To Love and To Cherish

Baby Shower Page

Finished Size: 12" square

Quilling Materials:

Note: Refer to Quilling Tools and Supplies on pages 12–15.

- $1/8$"-wide quilling papers:

    Bright white
    Cadet blue
    Lavender
    Pink
    Rose pink
    Seafoam green
    Sky blue
    Yellow

- Graph paper

- Paper crimper

- Scratch paper

Quilling Instructions:

Note: Refer to Quilling Techniques on pages 18–25.

Quill $7/8$"-tall "BABY," using pink for the two Bs and sky blue for the A and Y.

Pacifier: Quill 3" green marquise.

Quill $1\frac{1}{2}$" green loose circle. Insert quilling tool in center of circle and further loosen rolls.

Quill $2\frac{1}{2}$" yellow teardrop. Pinch again $1/8$" away from first point. Adhere flat section of teardrop to one side of marquise and loose circle to other side of marquise to form pacifier.

Rattle: Quill 3" lavender loose circle.

Quill $1\frac{1}{2}$" green loose circle. Insert quilling tool in center and further loosen rolls.

Adhere $1/4$" strip between circles to form rattle.

Woven umbrella: *Note: refer to quilling instructions for the Woven Umbrella instructions on pages 32–33.* Tear twenty-two 3" white, ten 3" rose, and ten 3" medium blue strips.

Page Materials:

- Cardstocks:

    Medium pink
    White

- Computer/color printer or marker

- Papers:

    Diamond print
    Medium blue

- Corner edgers

- Corner rounder

- Markers: light blue, pink

Page Instructions:

Print "PINK or BLUE May your wish come true" on $8\frac{1}{2}$" x 11" white cardstock. *Note: If computer and printer are not available, hand-print words with marker. Trim to desired size.*

Use corner edgers on wording piece, cardstocks, and papers. Draw dashed lines with markers as shown in photograph, or as desired.

Round corners of square photo and cardstock piece of choice as shown, or as desired.

Layer and adhere cardstock, paper, photos, and wording as shown, or as desired.

Arrange and adhere woven umbrella on wording piece and quilled letters with pacifier and rattle to front of page as shown, or as desired.

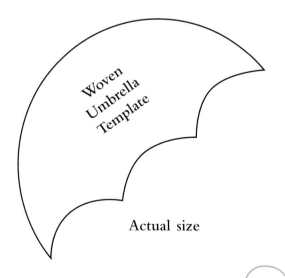

Woven Umbrella Template

Actual size

PINK or BLUE
May your wish come true

BABY

New Baby Page

Finished Size: 12" square

Quilling Materials:

Note: Refer to Quilling Tools and Supplies on pages 12–15.

- $1/8$"-wide quilling papers:

  Lavender

  Periwinkle

  Pink

  Seafoam green

  Yellow

Quilling Instructions:

Note: Refer to Quilling Techniques on pages 18–25.

Quill $7/8$"-tall periwinkle "BABY BOY" twice.

Quill two 3" pink hearts.

 Foot (make 2): Quill 9" yellow loose circle. Squeeze bottom third to shape arch of foot. Adhere rolls together inside inden tation and pin until dry.

Quill one 2" and four 1" yellow tight circles for toes.

Pacifier: Quill 6" green marquise.

Quill 3" green loose circle. Insert quilling tool in center of circle and further loosen rolls.

Quill 4" lavender teardrop. Pinch again $3/16$" away from first point. Adhere flat section of teardrop to one side of marquise and loose circle to other side of marquise to form pacifier.

Rattle: Quill 6" pink loose circle.

Quill 3" green loose circle. Insert quilling tool in center of 3" circle and further loosen rolls.

Cut $3/8$" green strip. Adhere strip between circles to form rattle.

Page Materials:

- Cardstocks:

  Dark blue

  Light blue

  White

- Papers:

  Medium blue

- Decorative-edged scissors: mini-scallop

Page Instructions:

Trim 20 medium blue $1^3/4$" squares with mini-scallop scissors.

Layer and adhere cardstocks, baby picture, four white $1^3/8$" squares, sixteen blue $1^3/8$" squares, and scallop-edged squares to page as shown in photograph, or as desired.

Adhere letters, hearts, feet, toes, pacifier, and rattle to page as shown, or as desired.

Suggestion:

This page can be made for a baby girl by simply quilling "GIRL" instead of "BOY," and by changing the colors of quilling papers, cardstocks, and papers used. *Note: If quilling "GIRL", do not quill the two hearts. The two hearts will be replaced with the two "L" letters.*

Bath Page

Finished Size: 12" square

Quilling Materials:

Note: Refer to Quilling Tools and Supplies on pages 12–15.

- $1/8$"-wide quilling papers:

    Aqua

    Melon

    Yellow

- Paper crimper

Quilling Instructions:

Note: Refer to Quilling Techniques on pages 18–25.

Large duck (make 4): Quill 9" yellow teardrop for body. Flatten one side of teardrop slightly for bottom of body.

Quill $3^{1}/2$" yellow eccentric loose circle on needle tool for head.

Cut 3" yellow strip in half lengthwise and quill teardrop on needle tool for wing.

Cut $3/8$" melon strip and fold in half to form beak. Adhere shapes together as shown in photograph.

Medium duck (make 8): Make same as large duck with 6" teardrop for body, $2^{1}/2$" eccentric loose circle for head, 2" teardrop for wing, and $5/16$" strip for beak.

Small duck (make 4): Make same as large duck with $4^{1}/2$" teardrop for body, 2" eccentric loose circle for head, $1^{1}/2$" teardrop for wing, and $1/4$" strip for beak.

Crimp two aqua strips quilling paper. Cut to form lengths that will fit around mounted bath photo as shown in photograph.

Quill four 3" aqua eccentric loose circles.

Page Materials:

- Cardstocks:

    Aqua

    Dark aqua

    Gold

    Yellow

- Papers:

    Light blue

    Water print

- Alphabet stencil: 1"-tall letters

- Corner edgers

- Petite glass beads: black

Page Instructions:

Use corner edgers on paper and cardstock as shown in photograph, or as desired. *Note: $8^{1}/2$" x $1^{1}/2$" light blue paper and $8^{3}/4$" x $1^{3}/4$" dark aqua cardstock was used for this scrapbook page.* Layer and adhere.

With alphabet stencil, trace "BATH TIME" onto dark aqua cardstock and cut out. Layer and adhere as shown, or as desired.

Layer and adhere cardstocks, papers, "BATH TIME" quote, and photograph to page as shown, or as desired.

Arrange and adhere ducks, crimped strips, and eccentric loose circles around photo as shown. Adhere one glass bead to center of eccentric coil on duck heads for eyes.

Suggestion:

Stencil the baby's name instead of "Bath Time."

Birthday Page

Finished Size: 12" square

Quilling Materials:

Note: Refer to Quilling Tools and Supplies on pages 12–15.

- ⅛"-wide quilling papers:

    Bright yellow
    Holiday green
    True red
    Violet

Quilling Instructions:

Note: Refer to Quilling Techniques on pages 18–25.

Cake: Quill six 12" yellow squares. Adhere together in two rows of three.

Icing: Quill three 3" red S-scrolls.

Quill four 3" green S-scrolls.

Candle: Quill ³⁄₁₆" x ¾" rectangle from 9" strip violet quilling paper.

Quill 3" yellow teardrop for flame.

Optional: Quill two ³⁄₁₆" x ½" rectangles from 6" strips violet quilling paper.

Quill two 3" yellow teardrops for flames.

Adhere shapes together as shown in photograph.

Page Materials:

- Cardstocks:

    Dark blue
    White

- Alphabet stencil: 1"-tall letters

- Corner rounder

- Ink pad: dark blue

- Large dot stencil

- Markers: black, blue, green, red, yellow

- Sponge dauber

Suggestion:

Try making a balloon bouquet of quilled teardrops with squiggly lines drawn in to emulate string.

Page Instructions:

Sponge large dots on white background cardstock with large dot stencil, ink pad, and sponge dauber.

Cut four 1¼"-squares from white cardstock. Cut squares in half diagonally to make eight triangles total.

Cut lengths of quilling paper and adhere to triangles as shown in photograph, cutting two colors in half lengthwise to ¹⁄₁₆"-wide. Trim quilling papers as needed.

Using alphabet stencil, trace "Happy Birthday" onto white cardstock with black marker and fill in with colored markers. Cut out, leaving a ⅛" border. Layer and adhere to cardstock of desired color. Trim edges, leaving ⅛" border.

Round cardstock corners as shown, or as desired.

Layer and adhere cardstocks, "Happy Birthday," photo corners, and photos as shown, or as desired.

Cut ⅛" squares from four colors of quilling paper, about thirteen of each color. Arrange and adhere close to edges of rounded white cardstock to form border. Adhere quilled cake inside border.

Happy First Birthday

Suggestion:

Use colors, patterns, etc., that are in
your photos to customize the page.

Dog Page

Finished Size: 12" square

Quilling Materials:

Note: Refer to Quilling Tools and Supplies on pages 12–15.

- $\frac{1}{8}$"-wide quilling papers:

    Black

    Celestial blue sparkling

Quilling Instructions:

Note: Refer to Quilling Techniques on pages 18–25.

Quill $\frac{7}{8}$"-tall blue "Buddies."

Large paw print (make 2): Quill 9" black triangle with rounded points. Round one side.

Quill four 3" black loose circles. Squeeze sides into oval shape.

Small paw print (make 2): Quill 6" black triangle with rounded points. Round one side.

Quill four 2" black loose circles. Squeeze sides into oval shape.

Page Materials:

- Cardstocks:

    Black

    Tan

    Textured black

- Papers:

    Paw-print stripes

    Shiny silver

- $\frac{1}{8}$"-diameter hole punch

- Corner rounder

- Marker: black

- Scratch paper

Page Instructions:

Round corners of cardstock pieces and photos. Layer and adhere cardstock and photos to page as shown in photograph, or as desired.

Trace Buckle, Dog Tag, and Ring Templates onto scratch paper, and cut out. Trace cutouts onto shiny silver paper and cut out. Punch a hole in top center of dog tag as per template. Write dog name(s) on tag with marker.

Adhere three 1" x $\frac{1}{8}$" shiny silver paper strips into a chain with one end link adhered through hole in dog tag. Slip other end link over one end of ring.

Punch three holes from scraps of scratch paper, cut out, and set aside.

Adhere $1\frac{1}{4}$"-wide textured black cardstock strip to top of page. Adhere letters, buckle, ring, and three holes onto cardstock strip to form collar as shown in photograph. *Note: Only adhere center of buckle above and below collar to page, in order to maintain a somewhat three-dimensional look. Likewise, only adhere straight edges of ring above and below collar to page, and allow dog tag to dangle.*

Arrange and adhere paw prints to page as shown in photograph.

Ring Template

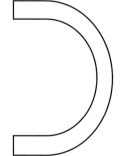

Buckle Template

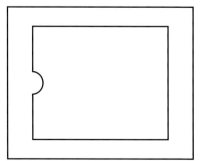

Dog Tag Template

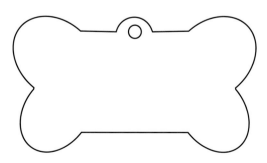

Actual size

Buddies

Frankie
and Paco

Suggestion:

If your dog photos have only one dog in
them, quill the words "My Buddy" and
write the dog's name on the dog tag.

Music Page

Finished Size: 12" square

Quilling Materials:

Note: Refer to Quilling Tools and Supplies on pages 12–15.

- $\frac{1}{8}$"-wide quilling paper: Black

Quilling Instructions:

Note: Refer to Quilling Techniques on pages 18–25.

D: Fold 4" strip at $2\frac{5}{8}$". Curve short end inward and roll long end $1\frac{3}{4}$" outward, forming a circle. Adhere circle to straight part of strip.

Pinch circle where adhered, to emulate musical note as shown in photograph. Adhere curved end where long end and circle are adhered.

O: Roll $3\frac{3}{4}$" strip $1\frac{5}{8}$" on one end, forming a circle. Adhere circle to strip and pinch circle where adhered.

Curve remainder of strip inward, and adhere long end to outside of pinched circle.

R: Fold 4" strip in opposite directions at $2\frac{5}{8}$" and $3\frac{3}{8}$". Roll long end $1\frac{3}{4}$" outward, forming a circle. Adhere circle to center, or straight, part of strip.

Pinch where adhered. Curve middle section inward. Adhere remaining fold to center of straight part of strip.

E: Fold $3\frac{1}{2}$" strip at $\frac{1}{2}$" and $1\frac{1}{4}$". Roll long end $1\frac{3}{4}$" outward, forming circle. Adhere circle to strip.

Pinch circle where adhered. Adhere $\frac{1}{2}$" strip to center of middle section of strip.

M: Fold $6\frac{3}{4}$" strip in half. Fold each half $\frac{7}{8}$" away from previous folds, in opposite directions. Roll each end $1\frac{3}{4}$" outward, forming circles.

Adhere circles to strips. Pinch circles where adhered.

I: Fold 3" strip at $\frac{1}{4}$" and 1". Roll long end $1\frac{3}{4}$" outward, forming circle. Adhere circle strip.

Pinch circle where adhered. Fold $1\frac{1}{4}$" strip at $\frac{1}{4}$" and 1". Adhere middle sections of two strips together.

Treble clef (make 2, see Fig. 5A, on page 88):
Fold 3" strip at 1". Curve short end inward, and 1" of long end outward. Adhere ends to straight section with ends meeting on opposite sides of straight section $\frac{5}{8}$" from fold. Pin until dry.

Fold 2" strip at $\frac{3}{4}$". Roll long end $\frac{5}{8}$" outward. Curve short end outward. Adhere fold of both strips together and curved end to straight section of 3" strip $\frac{3}{8}$" from fold. Pin until dry.

Curve and adhere $\frac{1}{4}$" strip inside treble clef $\frac{3}{8}$" from fold.

Base lef (make 2): Roll $2\frac{1}{4}$" strip $\frac{5}{8}$" on one end. Curve remainder of strip inward, straightening at end.

Quill two 1" loose circles.

Whole note: Quill $1\frac{3}{4}$" loose circle. Insert quilling tool in center and further loosen rolls.

Middle C whole note: Quill $1\frac{3}{4}$" loose circle. Insert quilling tool in center and further loosen rolls. Adhere edge of two $\frac{1}{8}$" strips to opposite sides of note.

Quarter note (make 2): Roll $2\frac{1}{2}$" strip $1\frac{3}{4}$" on one end to form circle. Adhere circle to strip, and pinch where adhered.

Eighth note (make 2): Fold 3" strip at $\frac{1}{2}$". Roll long end $1\frac{3}{4}$" outward to form circle. Adhere circle to strip and pinch where adhered.

Curve $\frac{1}{2}$" end inward and pinch. Adhere at fold.

Sixteenth note (make 2): Fold 5" strip at $2\frac{1}{4}$" and $2\frac{3}{4}$". Roll one end $1\frac{1}{2}$" outward and other end $1\frac{5}{8}$" inward to form circles. Adhere circles to strips and pinch where adhered.

Adhere $\frac{1}{2}$" strip $\frac{1}{8}$" below horizontal bar joining notes. Pin until dry.

Angle bars slightly.

Continued on page 88

Continued from page 86

Page Materials:

- Cardstocks:

    Black
    Blue
    White
    Yellow

- Decorative-edged scissors: deckle

- Facial tissues

- Ink pads: turquoise, yellow

- Marker: black

- Scratch paper

Page Instructions:

Staff lines: Make seven sections of five staff lines apiece with marker. *Note: Mine are placed $1/4$" from the left and right margins, $11/16$" from top and bottom margins, with $1/4$" between staff lines, and $1/4$" between staff sections.*

Deckle edges of staff-lined cardstock. Randomly ink cardstock by applying turquoise with a scrunched up facial tissue; repeat with yellow.

Trace Musical Note Template onto scratch paper and cut out. Trace Photo Templates onto backs of photos (two large and one small) and cut out. Layer and adhere photos to cardstock. Cut out, leaving $3/16$" to $1/4$" borders on all layers and including tails for musical notes as shown in photograph on page 87.

Arrange and adhere mounted photos, quilled letters, musical notes, and symbols to page. Adhere $3/16$"-wide black strips diagonally between tails of two mounted photos, trimming strips as needed.

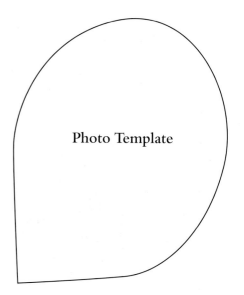

Photo Template

Enlarge 135%

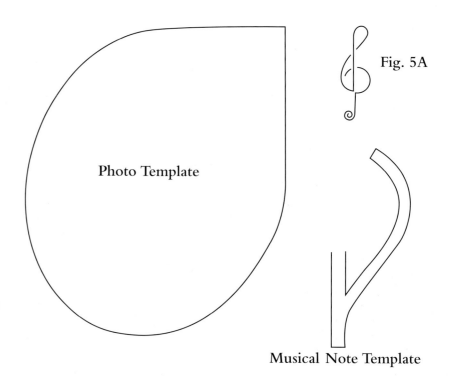

Fig. 5A

Photo Template

Musical Note Template

School Days Page

School Days Page

This page can be a work in progress. Assemble the page and add your child's school photo each year to the appropriate place on the page.

Finished Size: 12" square

Quilling Materials:

Note: Refer to Quilling Tools and Supplies on pages 12–15.

- $1/8$"-wide quilling papers:

  Black
  Bright white
  Holiday green
  Light gray
  Meadow green
  True red
  Twilight gold sparkling

- Cardstocks:

  Black
  Red
  White

Quilling Instructions:

Note: Refer to Quilling Techniques on pages 18–25.

Trace three Schoolhouse Templates onto scratch paper and cut out.

Schoolhouse: Adhere twenty-three red quilling strips to 3"-square red cardstock, so that strips touch but do not overlap.

Trace Schoolhouse Entrance Template with Schoolhouse Main Template surrounding it onto back of cardstock, so that strips run parallel to base. *Note: Bottom edge of entrance extends below bottom edge of main.* Cut out. Reapply any loose strips.

Schoolhouse steeple: Adhere ten 1" red strips to 1" x $1^1/2$" red cardstock, so that strips touch but do not overlap. Trace steeple template onto back of cardstock so that strips run parallel to base. Cut out and reapply any loose strips.

Roof: Adhere two overlapping $3/4$" black strips to steeple roof, 2" strips to main roof, and $1^1/4$" strips to entrance roof, as shown in photograph on page 89.

Schoolhouse steps: Center and adhere $3/4$" light gray strip above 1" light gray strip at base of entrance.

Door: Evenly adhere four $3/16$" white strips to $1/2$" x $3/8$" black cardstock to simulate window-panes. Center on $1^1/8$" x $1/2$" white cardstock $1/16$" below top edge.

Cut $1/2$" black strip in half length-wise to $1/16$" wide, and quill tight circle for doorknob. Adhere below window as shown. Center and adhere door above school-house steps.

Window (make 2): Evenly adhere four $1/4$" white strips to $5/8$" x $3/8$" black cardstock. Adhere to schoolhouse as shown.

Shrubs: Quill two 9" holiday green half circles with $1/2$" base, using 6" hole in quilling designer board. Shape into shrubs by pinching more on one end. Adhere beneath windows.

Bell: Quill 3" gold half circle with $1/4$" base. Pinch corners to shape bottom edges of bell.

Quill $1/2$" gold tight circle for clapper. Adhere clapper to bottom of bell.

Quill black "School Days" on needle tool, making letters $5/8$" and $3/8$" tall as follows:

S: Roll ends of $2^1/2$" strip to middle in opposite directions. Unroll slightly to form "S."

c: Roll ends of 2" strip $1/2$"–$5/8$" and curve middle inward.

h: Roll ends of $1^1/2$" strip $3/8$"–$1/2$" to make $5/8$" long. Roll ends of $1^1/4$" strip $1/4$" in opposite directions. Curve one end inward by roll.

o (make 2): Roll one end of $1^1/2$" strip $3/8$". Curve remainder of strip inward.

l: Roll ends of $1^1/2$" strip $3/8$"–$1/2$" in opposite directions to make $5/8$" long.

D: Roll ends of 1¹/₂" strip ³/₈"–¹/₂" to make ⁵/₈" long. Roll ends of 2" strip ³/₈"–¹/₂" and curve middle inward.

a: Roll ends of 1¹/₄" strip ³/₈"–¹/₂" to make ³/₈" long. Roll ends of 2" strip ¹/₂"–⁵/₈" and curve middle inward.

y: Roll ends of 2" strip ³/₈"–¹/₂" in opposite directions. Curve one end inward. Roll ends of 1¹/₄" strip ¹/₄" in opposite directions. Curve one end inward.

s: Roll ends of 2" strip to middle in opposite directions. Unroll slightly to form "s."

Apple (make 5): Quill 6" red loose circle. Indent top and bottom to form apple.

Quill 2" meadow green marquise for leaf. Quill 1" meadow green triangle with one ¹/₁₆" side and two ³/₁₆" sides for stem. Adhere leaf and stem to top of apple.

Page Materials:

- Cardstocks:
    Dark blue
    Light blue
    White
- Computer/color printer or marker
- Scratch paper

Page Instructions:

Layer white, dark blue, and light blue cardstocks and adhere to page as desired. *Note: I used 6" x 5" white, 5³/₄" x 4³/₄" dark blue, and 5¹/₂" x 4¹/₂" light blue cardstock pieces for my page.*

Trim school photos to 1¹/₂" x 2". Adhere to 1³/₄" x 2¹/₄" white cardstock.

Print school grades (1st, 2nd, 3rd, etc.) on white cardstock in black. *Note: If computer and printer are not available, hand-print grades with marker.* Trim to ⁵/₈" x ¹/₂".

Adhere cardstock pieces, available photos, school grades, schoolhouse, and other quilled shapes to page as shown in photograph on page 89, or as desired.

Actual size

Steeple Template

Schoolhouse Entrance Template

Schoolhouse Main Template

Baseball Page

Finished Size: 12" square

Quilling Materials:

Note: Refer to Quilling Tools and Supplies on pages 12–15.

- 1/8"-wide quilling papers:
    Black
    Bright white
    Tan

Quilling Instructions:

Note: Refer to Quilling Techniques on pages 18–25.

Baseball (make 4): Quill 2" white loose circle.

Bat (make 4): Quill 3/16" x 1 1/4" tan rectangle from 23" strip, using largest hole on quilling designer board. Squeeze long sides of rectangle 1/4" away from one end.

Wrap and adhere 5/8" tan strip around squeezed end, 1/8" away from end to form neck of bat. Trim excess.

Quill 7/8"-tall black "PLAY BALL."

Page Materials:

- Cardstocks:
    Black
    Cardboard brown
    Green
    Red
    White
- Marker: red
- Scratch paper

Page Instructions:

Cut two 5 3/4" green squares diagonally in half. Adhere four triangles to corners of background cardstock, leaving 1/4" border as shown in photograph.

Diagonally adhere four 2 1/4" white squares to page, aligning edges with triangles. Adhere 1 1/8"-wide white cardstock strips between squares to form baseball diamond border as shown.

Trace templates onto scratch paper; cut out. Using Small Circle cutout, trace white cardstock baseball; cut out. Using Large Circle cutout, trace four cardstock circles; cut out. *Note: Colors of larger cardstock circles can match player's team uniform.*

Line up baseball stitching template on top of baseball. Trace curves and add short angled stitching lines with marker as shown.

Center and draw 2"-square window on 3"-square scratch paper. Carefully cut out and discard 2" center. Use 2" window as a template to outline four baseball photos on the diagonal; cut out.

Adhere cardstock cutouts, photos, baseball, and quilled pieces to page as shown, or as desired.

Large Circle Template

Small Circle Template

Baseball Stitching Template

Actual size

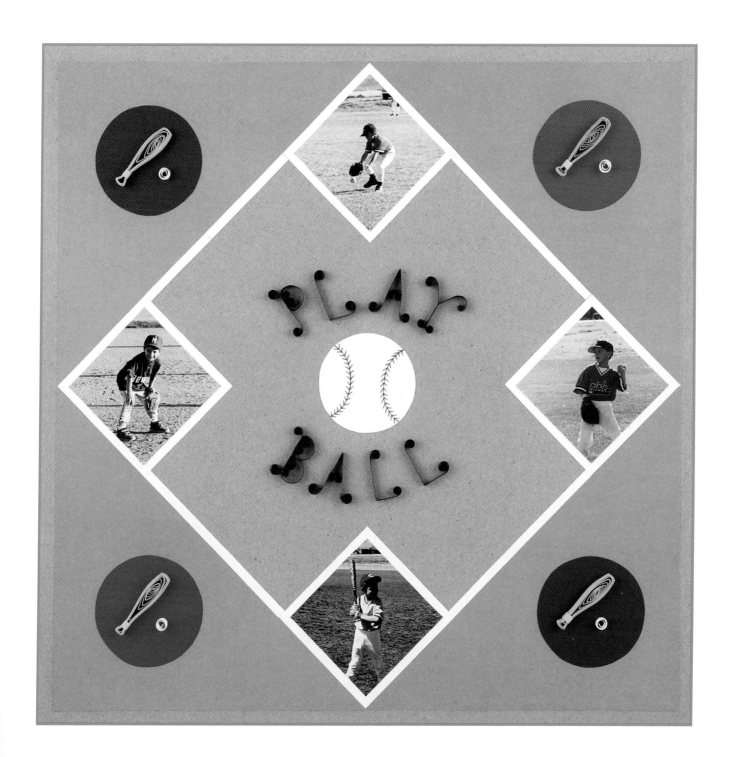

Suggestion:

This page layout works well with smaller photos in which the baseball player is 1"–2" tall.

Fishing Page

Finished Size: 12" square

Quilling Materials:

Note: Refer to Quilling Tools and Supplies on pages 12–15.

- $1/8$"-wide quilling papers:
    Celestial blue sparkling
    Leaf green
    Lincoln green
    Robin brown
    White/silver gilded edge
- $1/16$"-wide quilling papers:
    Black
    Bright white
- Cardstock:
    Blue
- Paper:
    Shiny silver
- Round toothpick
- Sewing needle
- Sewing thread

Quilling Instructions:

Note: Refer to Quilling Techniques on pages 18–25.

Short cattail (make 3): Quill 4" robin brown loose circle. Squeeze into a long oval to form cattail.

Cut 1" Lincoln green strip for stem. Adhere stem to end of cattail.

Cut two $1^{1}/4$" leaf green strips and two 1" Lincoln green strips for leaves.

Cut top $1/4$" of each leaf into a point and curve strips. Adhere bottom of $1^{1}/4$" leaves, then 1" leaves to bottom sides of stem as shown in photograph.

Tall cattail (make 2): Make same as short cattails with 4" loose circle for cattail, $1^{1}/4$" strip for stem, two $1^{1}/2$" strips, and two 1" strips for leaves.

Small fish: Quill 3" white/silver gilded edge eccentric loose circle in 3" strip hole on quilling designer board. Remove circle and squeeze into oval shape so that adhered end forms the head with eye and other end is the body.

Quill 1" white/silver gilded edge triangle for tail.

Quill two $3/4$" white/silver gilded edge triangles with one $1/16$" side and two $1/8$" sides for fins. Adhere shapes together to form fish as shown.

Medium fish: Make same as small fish with 6" eccentric loose circle in 6" strip hole on quilling designer board for body, 2" triangle for tail, and two 1" triangles with one $1/8$" side and two $3/16$" sides for fins.

Large fish: Make same as small fish with 9" eccentric loose circle in 9" strip hole on quilling designer board for body, 3" triangle for tail, and two $1^{1}/2$" triangles with one $3/16$" side and two $1/4$" sides for fins.

Fishing pole: Roll $2^{1}/2$" edge of $2^{1}/2$" x $1/2$" shiny silver paper around toothpick. Remove toothpick and adjust roll with fingers so pole is tapered at top end. Adhere edges.

Roll $3/8$" edge of $3/8$" x $1/2$" blue cardstock piece around toothpick to form fishing pole handle. Adhere roll $1/16$" from wider end of pole.

Quill 4" celestial blue tight circle for reel.

Cut two $1/2$" celestial blue strips lengthwise in half to form four $1/16$" x $1/2$" strips; quill one tight circle and three loose circles on needle tool. Set loose circles aside.

Quill $1/4$" celestial blue tight circle from $1/8$"-wide strip. Adhere base of $1/16$"-wide tight circle to end side of $1/8$"-wide tight circle. Adhere opposite end of $1/8$"-wide circle to center top of reel (4" tight circle) to form crank. (See Fig. 3A on page 58)

Continued on page 96

Continued from page 94

Adhere reel to side of pole next to handle, and three loose circles at even intervals as shown.

Hook: Cut ¹/₂" white/silver gilded edge strip in half lengthwise to ¹/₁₆"-wide. Curve into hook shape with fingers and cut a point at that end.

Thread needle with 9" gray thread, carefully pierce hole in straight end of hook, and push needle through hook. Tie a square knot in hook end of thread, and place a drop of adhesive on thread to hold knot. Cut excess from short end of thread.

Pass needle through center of loose circles beginning at tapered end and remove needle from thread. Loop free end once around reel, adhere, and trim excess.

Quill ⁷/₈"-tall robin brown "Gone Fishing."

Bubble (make 9): Quill ¹/₂" white loose circle. Smooth out center with tweezers or quilling tool.

Worm: Quill 1" black spiral.

Page Materials:

- Cardstocks:
    Dark blue
    Dark green
    Light tan
    Medium blue
    Medium tan
    Purple
    Rust
- Paper:
    Fishing lure print
- Scratch paper

Page Instructions:

Trim photos to desired sizes and shapes, using Template if desired.

Layer and adhere cardstock, paper, and photos as shown in photograph on page 95, or as desired. To achieve sandy bank effect, simply tear cardstock pieces by hand before layering.

Adhere quilled cattails, letters, fish, bubbles, fishing pole, and worm to page as shown.

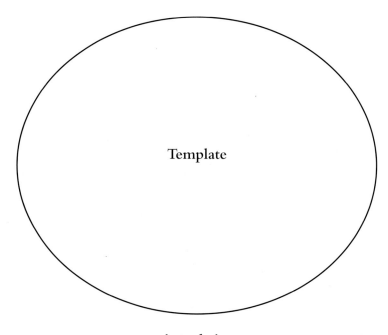

Template

Actual size

Camping Page

Camping Page

Finished Size: 12" square

Quilling Materials:

Note: Refer to Quilling Tools and Supplies on pages 12–15.

- $\frac{1}{8}$"-wide quilling papers:

  Brown

  Brown/rust two-toned

  Dark green/light green two-toned

  Dark yellow/light yellow two-toned

  Firecracker red sparkling

  Orange/yellow two-toned

  Oxford blue

  Red/light orange two-toned

  White/silver gilded edge

- $\frac{1}{4}$"-wide quilling paper:

  Bright white

- Cardstock:

  Brown

- Chalk: brown

- Cotton swab

- Decorative-edged scissors: deckle

Quilling Instructions:

Note: Refer to Quilling Techniques on pages 18–25.

Campfire: Roll long edges of $2\frac{1}{2}$" x $\frac{1}{2}$" and two 2" x $\frac{1}{2}$" brown cardstock pieces around toothpick for logs. Adhere edges together and remove toothpick.

Cut two 2" logs in half on the diagonal. Adhere diagonal cuts to center of $2\frac{1}{2}$" log, two above and two below as shown in photograph on page 97. Cut ends of logs with deckle scissors.

Tear 4" strip each of red/light orange, orange/yellow, and dark yellow/light yellow. Overlap and adhere strips together lengthwise with orange in center.

Quill 12" eccentric teardrop with red in center for large flame.

Quill two 9" eccentric teardrops, using 3" strip red/light orange, orange/yellow, and dark yellow/light yellow for small flames. Curve pinched end of small flames.

Adhere large flame above center of logs. Adhere two small flames layered over logs and large flame as shown.

Toasted marshmallow (make 2): Quill 2" white loose circle for marshmallow. Apply brown chalk to one side of marshmallow with cotton swab.

Quill 3" brown spiral for skewer. Bend slightly to resemble a branch. Adhere center of marshmallow to skewer about $\frac{1}{4}$" from one end of skewer.

Adhere toasted marshmallows above campfire as shown.

Pine tree (make 2): Quill 9" brown/rust triangle with one $\frac{3}{16}$" side and two $\frac{7}{8}$" sides for tree trunk.

Tear $1\frac{1}{2}$" brown/rust strip. Fold in half. Adhere fold together and to top $\frac{1}{8}$" of tree trunk.

Tear two $1\frac{1}{4}$" brown/rust strips. Fold in half and adhere to strip previously adhered to top of tree trunk.

Quill 2", 3", 4", and 5" dark green/light green V-scrolls, alternating light and dark on outside.

Adhere V-scrolls to top of tree trunk, starting with 5" V-scroll on bottom and ending with 2" V-scroll on top.

Lantern: Quill 1" firecracker red tight circle.

Quill $2\frac{1}{2}$" firecracker red half circle with $\frac{1}{4}$" base.

Quill 3" firecracker red rectangle with two $\frac{3}{8}$" sides and two $\frac{1}{8}$" sides.

Quill 6" white/silver gilded edge loose circle.

Quill $2\frac{1}{2}$" firecracker red rectangle with two $\frac{5}{16}$" sides and two $\frac{1}{8}$" sides.

Quill 7" firecracker red rectangle with two $\frac{1}{2}$" sides and two $\frac{5}{16}$" sides. Adhere shapes together in order from top to bottom as shown.

Cut $\frac{1}{2}$" firecracker red strip. Fold each end scant $\frac{1}{8}$". Bring folds together and flatten center against fold to form a "T" shape. (See Fig. 6A) Adhere bottom edge of "T" shape to right side of bottom rectangle for lantern valve.

Cut 2" strip firecracker red in half lengthwise. Curve middle and adhered ends to sides of rectangle to form handle.

Coffee pot: Quill 1" oxford blue tight circle.

Quill $2\frac{1}{2}$" oxford blue half circle with $\frac{5}{16}$" base.

Quill 9" oxford blue uneven marquise with one $\frac{13}{16}$" side. Pinch $\frac{1}{4}$" away from one point on shorter side and $\frac{3}{8}$" away from opposing point to form shape with $\frac{1}{4}$" top, $\frac{3}{8}$" bottom, and two $\frac{5}{8}$" diagonal sides. Adhere shapes together in order from top to bottom as shown.

Quill 2" oxford blue triangle with one $\frac{1}{8}$" side and two $\frac{1}{4}$" sides. Adhere one $\frac{1}{4}$" side of triangle to top left side of coffee pot for spout.

Cut $\frac{1}{2}$" oxford blue strip. Curve one end. Adhere curved end to top right side of coffee pot for handle.

Page Materials:

- Cardstocks:

    Black

    Brown

    Cardboard brown

    Gold

    Green

    Light tan

    Medium tan

    Mottled tan

    Red/orange

    Yellow

- Brown chalk

- Cotton swab

- Decorative-edged scissors: deckle

- Stickers: $\frac{7}{8}$"-tall log letters

- Water brush or sponge

Page Instructions:

Deckle edges of cardstock pieces and photos as shown in photograph. Apply chalk to desired edges with cotton swab.

Wet edges of cardstock to which "THE GREAT OUTDOORS" will be adhered. Tear edges. Layer and adhere. Apply log letter stickers.

Adhere cardstock, photos, and "THE GREAT OUTDOORS" piece to page as shown in photograph on page 97, or as desired.

Adhere all quilled shapes to page as shown, or as desired.

Fig. 6A

Graduation Page

Finished Size: 12" square

Quilling Materials:

Note: Refer to Quilling Tools and Supplies on pages 12–15.

- $1/8$"-wide quilling papers:

    Black

    Starlight silver sparkling

- $1/16$"-wide quilling paper:

    True red

- Papers:

    Light silver

    White

Quilling Instructions:

Note: Refer to Quilling Techniques on pages 18–25.

Cap: Quill 18" black diamond.

Quill 15" black uneven marquise with 1" side. Pinch shorter side halfway between points.

Quill $3/4$" black tight circle. Adhere diamond shape on top of curved side of uneven marquise and tight circle. *Note: Tight circle should be adhered under top point of diamond for stabilization.*

Tassel: Quill fringed flower with 1" x $1/4$" silver paper; do not spread fringe.

Cut 1" silver quilling strip into one $1/16$"-wide strip and two $1/32$"-wide strips. Adhere one $1/32$"-wide strip around uncut end of rolled fringed. Trim as needed.

Trim remaining $1/32$"-wide strip down to $3/4$"-long. Adhere one end to inside center of uncut edge of rolled fringe. Adhere other end diagonally to center of diamond as shown in photograph.

Roll $1/16$"-wide strip into a tight circle. Adhere tight circle to center of diamond on top of adhered end of $1/32$"-wide strip.

Scroll: Using needle tool, curve 2" x $1 1/4$" white paper along short side. Roll to $1/4$" diameter. Adhere rolls between first and second layers of scroll, where bow loops will cover adhered spot.

Bow loops: Loop ends of $1 3/4$" red strip to center and adhere. Wrap and adhere $1/4$" red strip vertically around center of bow loops. Trim excess as needed.

Bow tails: Overlap and adhere ends of two $1/2$" red strips in a V-shape. Trim other ends at an angle. Adhere overlapped ends to center back of bow loops.

Wrap and adhere 1" red strip around center of scroll. Trim as needed. Adhere bow to center of scroll.

Page Materials:

- Cardstocks:

    Black

    Dark blue

    Light blue

    White

- Papers:

    Dark silver

    Water print

- Decorative-edged scissors: deckle

- Ink pad: black

- Rubber stamp: "Congratulations"

Page Instructions:

Stamp "Congratulations" on $4 3/4$" x $3 1/2$" white cardstock. Layer and adhere to 5" x $3 3/4$" black cardstock.

Cut two $1 1/2$"-square cardstock pieces diagonally in half with deckle-edged scissors. Adhere 2" black strip to each triangle as shown in photograph. Trim as needed. Adhere to corners of mounted "Congratulations" piece.

Arrange and adhere cardstocks, paper, photos, and quilled pieces as shown, or as desired.

Suggestion:

Instead of stamping "Congratulations,"
use the space to display graduate's name,
date of graduation, place of graduation,
and degree earned.

Golf Page

Finished Size: 12" square

Quilling Materials:

Note: Refer to Quilling Tools and Supplies on pages 12–15.

- $1/8$"-wide quilling papers:
    Black
    Bright white
    Celestial blue sparkling
    Tan
    Yellow
- Cardstock:
    Black
- Paper:
    Dark shiny silver

Quilling Instructions:

Note: Refer to Quilling Techniques on pages 18–25.

Quill $3/4$"-tall black "Hole in One!" Substitute 12" white loose circle wrapped once with black quilling strip for the capital "O."

Golf club: Quill 3" celestial blue triangle with one $1/4$" side and two $3/8$" slightly rounded sides to form head of club.

Roll 2" edge of 2" x $1/2$" silver paper tightly and smoothly around toothpick to form shaft. Adhere edges together and remove toothpick.

Roll $1/2$"-square black cardstock around toothpick. Remove toothpick. Adhere around end of shaft. Adhere head of club to other end of shaft as shown in photograph.

Golf ball: Quill 2" white loose circle on needle tool.

Tee: Quill $1 1/2$" tan triangle with one $1/8$" side and two $3/16$" sides. Squeeze $3/16$" sides to form tee. Adhere $1/8$" side of tee to edge of ball.

Golf flag/pole: Roll 2" edge of 2" x $1/2$" black cardstock tightly and smoothly around toothpick to form pole. Adhere edges together, and remove toothpick.

Quill 6" yellow triangle with one $5/16$" side and two $9/16$" sides for flag. Adhere short side of flag to end of pole.

Page Materials:

- Cardstocks:
    Black
    Dark blue
    Dark green
    Light blue
    White
- Papers:
    Grass print
    Light green
    Tan
- $1/4$"-diameter hole punch
- Border stencil: large curve
- Corner rounder
- Ink pads: brown, green
- Round toothpick
- Rubber stamp: sand texture
- Scratch paper
- Sponge

Page Instructions:

Round corners of photos and cardstock pieces to which photos will be mounted.

Trace border stencil on cardstock and paper being used for fairway strip. Make sure stencil is consistently positioned so layers line up properly. Cut out curves.

Layer and adhere cardstock, paper, and photos to page as shown in photograph, or as desired.

Trace Golf Templates on page 104 to scratch paper and cut out. Trace cutouts onto cardstock or paper and cut out. Punch $1/4$" circle from cardstock.

Sponge green ink onto fairway. Stamp brown ink many times onto sand trap until desired look is achieved.

Arrange and adhere golf course pieces and punched circle together as shown, or as desired.

Arrange and adhere quilled letters, golf course, golf club, ball, and flag/pole to page.

Hole in One!

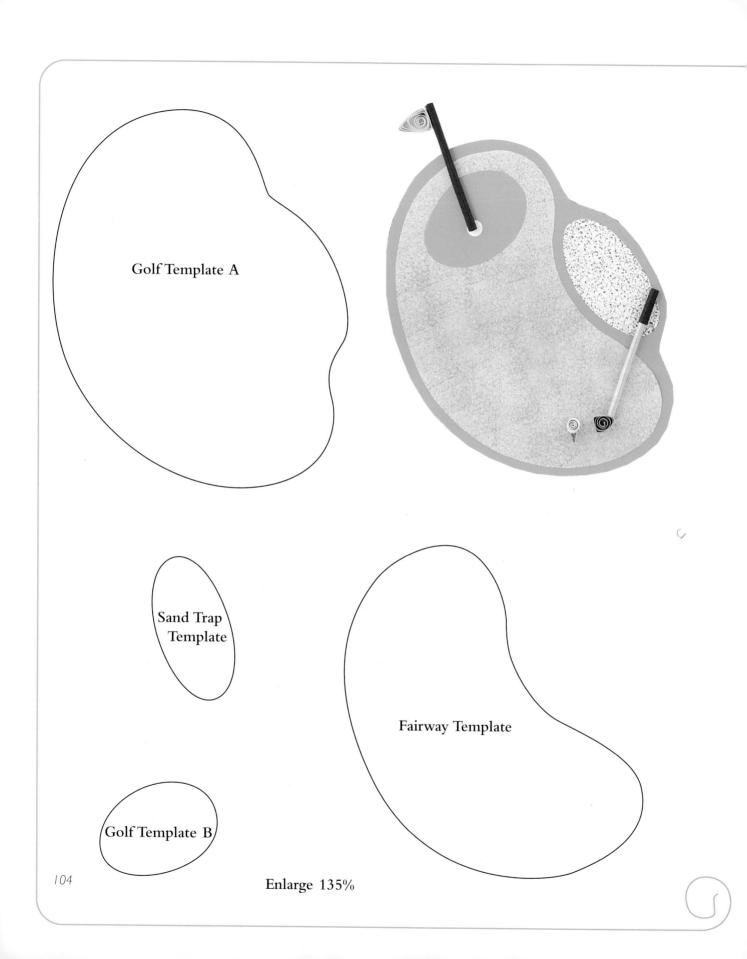

Golf Template A

Sand Trap
Template

Fairway Template

Golf Template B

Enlarge 135%

Vacation Page

Vacation Page

Finished Size: 12" square

Quilling Materials:

Note: Refer to Quilling Tools and Supplies on pages 12–15.

- $^1/_{16}$"-wide quilling papers:
  - Black
  - Bright white
  - True red
- Cardstocks:
  - Black
  - Red
  - White
  - Yellow
- Scratch Paper

Quilling Instructions:

Note: Refer to Quilling Techniques on pages 18–25.

Trace Sign Templates onto scratch paper and cut out.

No U-Turn sign: Lightly draw border $^1/_{16}$" away from edges of $1^3/_4$"-square white cardstock with pencil. Center Circle Template on white cardstock and lightly trace. Lightly draw diagonal line inside circle on white cardstock. Erase most of lines so they are very faint.

Curve 4" red strip with edge of quilling tool. Adhere edge of strip to circle a little at a time, overlapping and adhering ends.

Quill 5" black triangle. Curve 1" of $1^1/_2$" black strip with quilling tool. Shape with fingers as needed. Adhere triangle and curved strip to sign as shown.

Cut red strips the length of each drawn diagonal line segment between circle, triangle, and curved strip; adhere between quilled shapes. Fold $6^3/_4$" black strip in half. Fold again $1^5/_8$" away from center on each end.

Adhere edges of strip to drawn border one side at a time. Trim and adhere ends together.

STOP sign: Trace Stop Sign Template onto 2"-square red cardstock and transfer cut out. Center and trace "STOP" on sign. Adhere 8" white strip to edges, adhering and trimming one side at a time.

Quill "STOP" with white quilling paper as follows:

S: Curve halves of 1" strip in opposite directions with edge of quilling tool. Trim as needed.

T: Cut $^7/_{16}$" strip and $^3/_{16}$" strip.

O: Curve entire length of $1^1/_4$" strip with edge of quilling tool. Overlap and adhere ends.

P: Fold 1" strip at $^7/_{16}$". Curve long end inward.

Adhere quilled letters over transferred letters.

Merge sign: Lightly draw border $^1/_{16}$" away from edges of $1^3/_4$"-square yellow cardstock with pencil. Erase most lines so they are very faint. Fold $6^3/_4$" black strip in half. Fold again $1^5/_8$" away from first fold on each end.

Adhere edges of strip to drawn border one side at a time. Trim and adhere ends together.

Quill 5" black triangle.

Fold $1^1/_2$" black strip in half. Curve one half outward with edge of quilling tool.

Adhere strip together from fold halfway down. Arrange and adhere strip and triangle to sign as shown.

Center and adhere Merge sign and No U-Turn sign to 2"-square black cardstock pieces. Center and adhere stop sign to $2^1/_4$"-square black cardstock. Trim diagonal edges to same border width as horizontal and vertical edges.

Page Materials:

- Cardstocks:

  Black
  Bright White
  Dark brown
  Medium brown
  Reddish brown
  Sandstone

- Paper:

  Travel signs print

- Decorative-edged scissors: deckle

- Stickers: $7/8$"-tall log letters

- Water brush or sponge

Page Instructions:

Cut twenty $1/4$" white quilling strips. Adhere down center of 10" x $1^1/2$" black cardstock for road. Cut road into four pieces, if desired.

Wet edges of cardstock to which log letter stickers will be adhered. Tear edges. Layer and adhere on medium brown cardstock. Deckle edges.

Layer and adhere road, cardstock pieces, paper, log letter stickers, photos, and quilled signs to page as shown in photograph on page 105, or as desired.

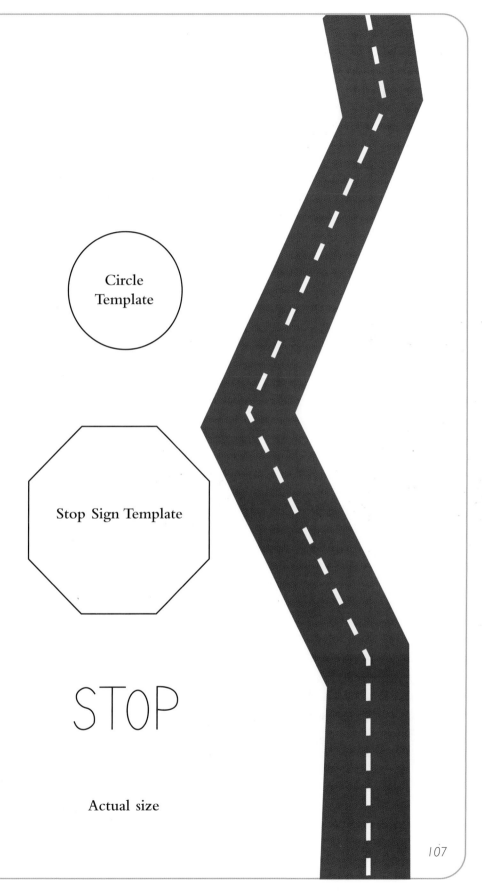

Circle Template

Stop Sign Template

STOP

Actual size

Beach Page

Finished Size: 12" square

Quilling Materials:

Note: Refer to Quilling Tools and Supplies on pages 12–15.

- $1/8$"-wide quilling papers:

    Bright yellow

    Soft ivory

    Tan

- Paper crimper

Quilling Instructions:

Note: Refer to Quilling Techniques on pages 18–25.

Sun: Quill 18" bright yellow loose circle.

Crimp 8" bright yellow strip with paper crimper and cut into twelve $1/2$" lengths for sunrays.

Footprint (make 3): Quill 6" tan loose circle. Squeeze bottom third to shape arch of foot. Adhere rolls inside indentation and pin until dry.

Quill one 1" and four $1/2$" tan tight circles for toes.

Bucket: Quill 15" bright yellow uneven marquise with one $1^1/8$" side and one $1^3/8$" side. Pinch short side $3/8$" from one pinch for bottom of bucket. Pinch long side $5/8$" from other pinch for top of bucket. *Note: Sides of bucket should be $3/4$"-long.*

Curve and adhere $1^1/2$" bright yellow strip to bucket to form handle.

Shovel: Quill 3" bright yellow half circle with $1/4$" straight edge.

Quill 2" bright yellow half circle with $3/16$" straight edge. Insert quilling tool in center of half circle and further loosen rolls.

Cut $1/4$" bright yellow strip. Adhere strip between curved edges of half circles to form shovel.

Seagulls: Cut two 1" and two $1^1/2$" ivory strips. Fold each strip in half. Curve both halves outward from fold to end using edge of slotted quilling tool.

Adhere center of strip together $1/8$" from fold. Bend one half of strip to one side to form flying birds.

Page Materials:

- Cardstocks:

    Dark tan

    Light tan

    Medium tan

    Navy blue

    Turquoise

- Paper:

    Water print

- Decorative-edged scissors: wave

Page Instructions:

Trim photos as needed; adhere to cardstock trimmed with decorative-edged scissors.

Tear one long edge of 2"-wide light, medium, and dark tan cardstocks and 3"-wide water-print paper. Layer and adhere to page for sand and water.

Adhere mounted photos and quilled shapes to page as shown in photograph, or as desired.

Suggestion:

This page has ample room in the sand to add some journaling about your day at the beach.

Easter Egg Hunt Page

Finished Size: 12" square

Quilling Materials:

Note: Refer to Quilling Tools and Supplies on pages 12–15.

- 1/8"-wide quilling papers:
    Cadet blue
    Lavender
    Pink
    Seafoam green
    Tan
    Yellow
- Scratch paper
- Waxed paper
- Paper crimper

Quilling Instructions:

Note: Refer to Quilling Techniques on pages 18–25.

Basket: Trace Basket Template on page 112 to scratch paper, cut out, and place beneath waxed paper on quilling board.

Tear seven 2" tan strips. Line up one strip along right side, one strip along left side, and one strip vertically in center of

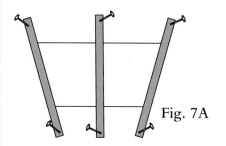

Fig. 7A

cutout. Edges of strips will overlap cutout; pin strips in place above and below basket outline. (See Fig. 7A)

Line up two strips vertically between center and each edge, equally spaced and slightly slanted. Pin top edge in place above cutout.

Tear eight 3" tan strips. Weave strips one at a time horizontally over and under pinned vertical strips, starting at top of cutout and working to bottom. (See Fig. 7B)

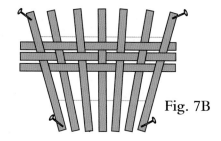

Fig. 7B

Adhere strips at any intersection in which a vertical strip overlaps a horizontal strip, removing and replacing pins as necessary. Make sure vertical strips remain slanted correctly. *Note: Vertical strips will have a space between them, but horizontal strips will be touching. Left and right vertical strips should stay lined up on edges of template.*

When all eight horizontal strips are woven and adhesive is dry, remove pins. Trim excess so that strips are even with edges of weaving. *Note: Basket should be about the size of the template.*

Adhere any loose edges or strips.

Handle: Tear one 10" tan strip. Fold each end back 1". Adhere edge of strip along side and bottom edges on back of basket, with folds at lower corners. Adhere overlapped ends together.

Quill six 1½" tan tight circles. Adhere to back of basket: one in each corner and two spaced across center for support.

Eggs: Quill two 6" loose circles in the following colors: pink, lavender, seafoam green, yellow.

Quill one 6" cadet blue loose circle. Squeeze all circles lightly to form egg shapes.

Bow (make 1 in each color used for eggs): Tear 2½" strip. Curve each half on quilling tool (similar to curling ribbon on scissors) and adhere ends to back center of strip to form loops. Wrap ½" strip vertically around center and adhere. Trim excess.

Tear two 1" strips for tails. Cut notch in one end of each strip. Overlap and adhere other ends in V-shape. Adhere overlap to center back of loops.

Decorated egg: Trace Decorated Egg Template onto scratch paper and cut out. Trace cutout onto cardstock and cut out.

Continued on page 112

Continued from page 110

Crimp 4" lengths of five colors used for eggs. Arrange and adhere one edge of crimped strips on egg shape as shown in photograph on page 111; trim excess.

Quill three 3" pink teardrops.

Quill five 3" yellow loose circles.

Quill four 3" seafoam green S-scrolls.

Quill five 3" cadet blue marquises.

Quill five 2" lavender hearts.

Adhere quilled pieces on egg shape as shown.

Page Materials:

- Cardstocks:
    Pastel plaid
    Pink
    White
    Yellow
- Papers:
    Lavender
    Light green
    Light pink
    Medium blue
- Decorative-edged scissors: mini-scallop, ripple
- Ink pad: pink
- Rubber stamp: "Happy Easter"
- Scratch paper

Page Instructions:

Trace Large Egg Template onto scratch paper; cut out. Trace cutout onto back of three photos; cut out.

Adhere photos and decorated egg to various colors of paper. Trim with decorative-edged scissors of choice, leaving $1/4$" border.

Stamp "Happy Easter" on $1\frac{1}{8}$" x $7/8$" white cardstock. Adhere to $1\frac{1}{2}$" x $1\frac{1}{4}$" light pink paper.

Trim edges of 3" x $4\frac{1}{4}$" white cardstock and $3\frac{3}{4}$" x 5" medium blue paper with decorative-edged scissors. Layer and adhere together. Adhere basket to layered cardstock as shown in photograph on page 111 with five eggs adhered behind top edge of basket. Adhere bow to front of basket.

Adhere cardstock, paper, layered "Happy Easter" piece, mounted photos, and quilled pieces to page as shown, or as desired.

Basket Template

Decorated Egg Template

Large Egg Template

Enlarge 150%

Halloween Page

Finished Size: 12" square

Quilling Materials:

Note: Refer to Quilling Tools and Supplies on pages 12–15.

- $1/8$"-wide quilling papers:

    Black

    Bright white

    Bright yellow

    Holiday green

    Orange

Quilling Instructions:

Note: Refer to Quilling Techniques on pages 18–25.

Candy corn (make 5): Quill $2^{1}/_{2}$" white triangle with one $1/4$" side and two $1/4$" slightly rounded sides.

Quill 4" bright yellow loose circle. Pinch into trapezoid with $1/4$" top, $1/4$" sides, and $3/8$" bottom.

Quill 5" orange loose circle. Pinch into trapezoid with $3/8$" top, $3/16$" sides, and $1/2$" bottom. Adhere and pin three shapes together until dry.

Pumpkin (make 4): Quill $7^{1}/_{2}$" orange loose circle. Slightly indent adhered spot to form pumpkin shape.

Quill 2" green triangle with one $3/16$" side and two $1/4$" sides. Curve one long side slightly to form stem. Adhere $3/16$" side of stem to

indented area of pumpkin. Pin together until adhesive dries.

Bat (make 3): Quill two 4" black marquises. Pinch two points on one side of each marquise to form wings.

Quill 4" black loose circle. Pinch two ears about $1/4$" apart to form head. Adhere wings to sides of head.

Spider: Quill 6" black loose circle for body and 4" black tight circle for head.

Cut eight 1" black strips for legs. Fold each strip in half. Fold back $1/8$" on one end of each strip for feet. On other end of strips, trim off $3/16$" on two strips, $1/8$" on two strips, and $1/16$" on four strips.

Page Materials:

- Cardstocks:

    Black

    Deep yellow

    Green

    Orange

    White

- Alphabet stencil: 1"-tall letters

- Decorative-edged scissors: deckle

- Marker: black

- Scratch paper

Page Instructions:

Trace Pumpkin and Stem Templates onto scratch paper and cut out. Trace pumpkin cutouts onto backs of two photos and cut out. Adhere to orange cardstock and cut out, leaving a $1/4$" border.

Trace stem cutout twice onto green cardstock and cut out. Adhere stems to tops of pumpkins, overlapping on back slightly.

Deckle edges of 2"-wide black cardstock strip. Layer and adhere $1^{1}/_{2}$"-wide white cardstock strip, $1^{3}/_{16}$" x $1^{1}/_{4}$" orange and yellow cardstock pieces, and 1" x $^{15}/_{16}$" black cardstock pieces as shown in photograph on page 113, or as desired. Adhere photo pumpkins to page.

Using alphabet stencil, trace "TRICK or TREAT" letters on cardstock and cut out. Adhere letters to page.

Arrange and adhere spider parts to page with shortest legs at bottom and longest legs at top as shown. With black marker, draw string above spider on page.

Arrange and adhere other quilled shapes to page as shown, or as desired.

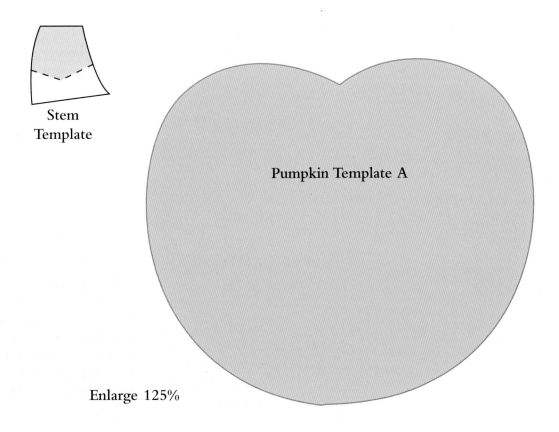

Stem
Template

Pumpkin Template A

Enlarge 125%

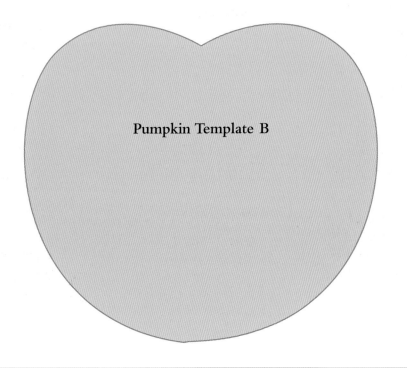

Pumpkin Template B

Thanksgiving Page

Finished Size: 12" square

Quilling Materials:

Note: Refer to Quilling Tools and Supplies on pages 12–15.

- $1/16$"-wide quilling papers:
  - Beech brown
  - Black
  - Bright white
  - Garnet
  - Lichen green
  - Robin brown
  - Tan
- $1/8$"-wide quilling paper:
  - Tan
- $1/4$"-wide quilling paper:
  - Bright white
- Cardstocks:
  - Brown
  - Gold
  - Olive green
  - Rust
- Bone folder
- Scratch paper

Quilling Instructions:

Note: Refer to Quilling Techniques on pages 18–25.

Leaves (make 3 rust, 1 brown, 3 olive green, and 2 gold):
Trace Leaf Templates on page 118 onto scratch paper and cut out.

Using bone folder, score pieces of green, rust, brown, and gold cardstock lengthwise down center. Fold in half.

Trace Narrow Leaf cutout onto green cardstock, Wide Leaf cutout onto gold cardstock, and Wavy-edged Leaf cutout onto brown and rust cardstocks, then cut out.

Cut diagonal slits in gold and green leaves $1/16$" apart from edges to center, stopping $1/16$" away from fold. Unfold leaves.

Turkey: Quill 17" beech brown loose circle in 15" hole on quilling designer board to form body.

Quill two 9" teardrops each from $1/16$"-wide green, garnet, robin brown, and tan strips for feathers. Pinch each teardrop again $1/8$" away from first point. Slightly squeeze teardrops, then position and adhere $1/8$" end of feathers to edges of body.

Quill two 3" robin brown half circles with $1/4$" base on needle tool for feet.

Cut four $1/4$" strips robin brown; adhere in a stack to thicken legs. Cut in half to $1/8$" long. Adhere feet and legs to bottom of body.

Curve 1" black strip on side of quilling tool for bow. Adhere both ends to center back of strip. Fold $1/2$" black strip in half. Adhere fold to center of loop strip. Adjust loops as needed.

Cut two $3/16$"-long strips of $1/4$"-wide white quilling paper. Overlap corners a little at an angle and adhere to form collar. Center and adhere edge of bow to collar. Adhere collar to body as shown in photograph.

Quill 15" beech brown loose circle in 12" hole on quilling designer board to form head.

Squeeze one-third of circle to form neck. Adhere between rolls and pin until dry. Slightly flatten base of neck, and adhere to collar just above bow.

Quill 3" robin brown triangle with two rounded corners on needle tool for beak.

Quill 3" garnet teardrop. Squeeze sides of teardrop and curve pointed end to form waddle.

Quill two 1" black tight circles for eyes. Wrap each eye with $1/16$"-wide white strip. Trim excess.

Quill 6" black quadrilateral shape with two parallel sides that are $3/8$" long and $1/4$" long, and two angled sides that are $3/8$" long for hat.

Continued on page 118

Continued from page 116

Cut 1½" black strip. Fold in half. Adhere halves together to form brim strip. Center and adhere long parallel side of quadrilateral to doubled brim strip. Pin until dry.

Cut ½" beech brown strip. Center and adhere strip to bottom of hat just above brim. Trim excess.

Cut ⅛" square from ⅛"-wide tan quilling paper. Center and adhere to beech brown strip above brim.

Position and adhere beak, waddle, eyes, and hat to head as shown.

Page Materials:

- Cardstocks:

  Brown
  Gold
  Olive green
  Pale yellow
  Rust
  Tan

- Alphabet stencil: 1"-tall letters

- Decorative-edged scissors: deckle

- Marker: brown

- Mulberry paper: burgundy

- Water brush or sponge

Page Instructions:

Deckle edges of 11" x 3" pale yellow cardstock. *Note: I cut the corners off my main cardstock piece and drew squiggly lines around the edges with marker after deckling for added detail.*

Trim photos as needed. Adhere to desired cardstock and trim edges with deckle scissors.

Wet and tear edges of mulberry paper with water brush or sponge.

Trace "We Give Thanks" with alphabet stencil onto brown cardstock and cut out letters.

Layer and adhere all cardstock pieces, photos, mulberry paper, lettering, paper, leaves, and quilled shapes to page as shown in photograph on page 117, or as desired.

Wide Leaf Template

Wavy-edged Leaf Template

Narrow Leaf Template

Actual size

Snowflake Page

Chris on Mingus Mountain in the snow.

Chris and his snowman in the back yard.

SNOW FUN

Snowflake Page

Finished Size: 12" square

Quilling Materials:

Note: Refer to Quilling Tools and Supplies on pages 12–15.

- $\frac{1}{8}$"-wide quilling paper:
    Bright white
- Scratch paper
- Waxed paper

Quilling Instructions:

Note: Refer to Quilling Techniques on pages 18–25.

Large snowflake: Trace Snowflake Template onto scratch paper and place beneath waxed paper on quilling board.

Quill six 3" marquises; adhere points together at center so one marquise follows each template line. (See Fig. 8A)

Quill six 3" V-scrolls; adhere straight sections together so V is closed. Adhere base of V to outer points of marquises. (See Fig. 8B)

Quill six 2" V-scrolls; adhere curves between marquises so V points away from center. (See Fig. 8C)

Quill six 3" hearts; adhere folded ends to curved ends of 3" V-scrolls. (See Fig. 8D)

Quill six 3" hearts, but do not adhere curves. Adhere inside of open rolls to pointed end of 2"

V-scrolls. (See Fig. 8E)

Quill six 2" teardrops; adhere pinched ends to rolled ends of closed hearts. (See Fig. 8F)

Medium snowflake: Assemble in same manner as large snowflake, using the following shapes: six 2" marquises, six 2" closed V-scrolls, six closed 1$\frac{1}{2}$" open V-scrolls, six 2" closed hearts, six 2" open hearts, six 1$\frac{1}{2}$" teardrops.

Page Materials:

- Cardstocks:
    Dark blue
    Medium blue
    White
- Paper:
    Light blue
- (12" x 1$\frac{1}{2}$") paper ribbon: white
- Ink pad: blue
- Marker: blue
- Snowflake punches: small, medium, large
- Sponge dauber
- Stencils: $\frac{3}{4}$"-tall alphabet letters, 2$\frac{1}{8}$"-diameter circle, 4$\frac{3}{4}$"-long oval, 3$\frac{7}{8}$"-long oval

Page Instructions:

Stencil "SNOW FUN" on light blue paper, using sponge dauber, ink pad, and alphabet stencil. Cut out letters, leaving a $\frac{1}{8}$" border.

Trace ovals onto back of photos and cut out. Adhere to dark blue cardstock and trim, leaving a $\frac{1}{8}$" border.

Trace circles onto white cardstock and cut out. Color edges of circles with sponge dauber and ink pad to make snowballs. Journal snowballs with marker. *Note: To keep journaling even, lightly pencil lines across snowballs with a pencil and ruler. Erase all pencil lines after journaling is complete.*

Punch snowflakes from cardstock. *Note: I used two large, three medium, and seven small snowflakes for my page.*

Cut 1$\frac{1}{2}$"-wide paper ribbon in half lengthwise.

Adhere paper ribbon, 2$\frac{3}{4}$"-wide dark blue cardstock strip, stenciled letters, snowballs, mounted photos, punched snowflakes, and quilled snowflakes to page as shown in photograph on page 119, or as desired.

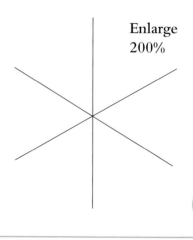

Enlarge
200%

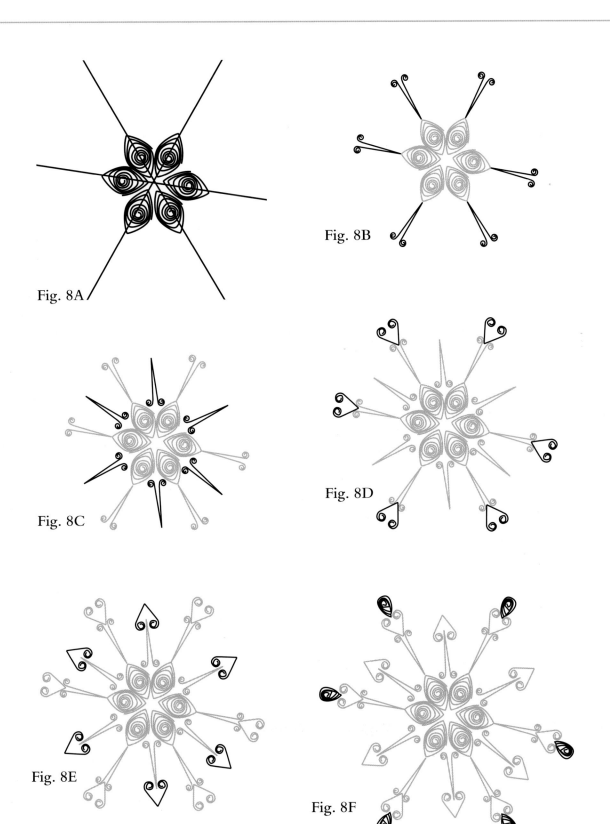

Fig. 8A

Fig. 8B

Fig. 8C

Fig. 8D

Fig. 8E

Fig. 8F

Christmas Page

Finished Size: 12" square

Quilling Materials:

Note: Refer to Quilling Tools and Supplies on pages 12–15.

- ⅛"-wide quilling papers:
    Bright yellow
    Celestial blue sparkling
    Holiday green
    True red

Quilling Instructions:

Note: Refer to Quilling Techniques on pages 18–25.

Christmas lights: Quill four 6" yellow teardrops.

Quill four 6" green teardrops.

Quill three 6" red teardrops.

Quill eleven 2½" blue bunny ears. Slightly flatten rounded part of bunny ears. Adhere curved edge of teardrops to curved edge of bunny ears.

Page Materials:

- ⅛"-wide quilling papers:
    Black
- Cardstocks:
    Green
    White
- Paper:
    Green print
- Alphabet stamps: ⅝"-tall
- Border stencils: large and small curve
- Die-cut stickers: snowflake
- Markers: black, blue, brown, green, red, yellow

Page Instructions:

Trace curvy stencil borders on two 1¾"-wide white cardstock strips and cut out. Make dots along edges, using black marker, if desired.

Draw wavy line down center of one border strip with large curve border stencil and black marker.

Working inch by inch, adhere edge of black quilling paper along line. Trim ends as necessary.

Color stamps with markers and huff on ink to moisten. Stamp "CHRISTMAS" on white cardstock. Darken any lighter areas with marker.

Center and draw 1"-square window on 2"-square white cardstock. Carefully cut out and discard 1"-square center. Use this as a template to lightly draw 1" square, centered around each letter. Cut out squares.

Draw colored lights around CHRISTMAS letters as shown in photograph, or as desired.

Layer and adhere all cardstock pieces, border strips, paper, photos, stickers, stamped letters, and quilled lights to page as shown, or as desired.

Acknowledgments

Delta/Rubber Stampede
(800) 423-4135
www.deltacrafts.com

Dolphin Enterprises
4677 Bonner Circle
Salt Lake City, UT 84117
(877) 910-3306 (toll free)
www.protect-a-page.com
www.dolphinenterprises.net

Duncan Enterprises/PSX
5673 East Shields Avenue
Fresno, CA 93727
(800) 438-6226 (toll free)
(559) 291-4444 (phone)
(559) 291-9444 (fax)
www.duncan-enterprises.com

Fiskars
7811 West Stewart Avenue
Wausau, WI 54401
(800) 500-4849
www.fiskars.com

Lake City Craft Co.
P.O. Box 2009
Nixa, MO 65714-2009
(417) 725-8444 (phone)
(417) 725-8448 (fax)
www.quilling.com

Plaid Enterprises/All Night Media
(800) 842-4197 (toll free)
www.plaidonline.com

Provo Craft
151 East 3450 North
Spanish Fork, UT 84660
(800) 937-7686 (toll free)
(801) 794-9006 (fax)
www.provocraft.com

Whimsiquills
25 Indian Run
Enfield, CT 06082
(877) 488-0894 (toll free)
(860) 749-0894 (phone)
(860) 763-3904 (fax)
www.whimsiquills.com

Special thanks go to my husband Jim, and my three sons Greg, Chris, and Nick, for all of their love, help, and patience with me while I worked on this book. A big thank-you goes to Cindy Stoeckl at Chapelle, Ltd., and her friend, Lauren Powell, without whom this book would not have been possible. My biggest thanks go to God for the talents, inspirations, opportunities, and blessings He has bestowed on me, both working on this book and in everyday life.

Credits

Book Editor: Ana Maria Ventura

Copy Editor: Marilyn Goff

Stylist: Kim Monkres

Photographer: Zac Williams

Book Designer: Dan Emerson
Pinnacle Marketing
Ogden, UT

About the Author

Susan Lowman has been making arts and crafts since childhood, when she took art classes every year in her junior and senior high schools. She enjoys paper quilling, crocheting, tatting, cross-stitching, paper crafts, and many more. Susan lives in Arizona with her husband, and their three sons. She has been a craft designer since 1998.

Metric Equivalency Charts

mm–millimeters   cm–centimeters
inches to millimeters and centimeters

inches	mm	cm	inches	cm	inches	cm
⅛	3	0.3	9	22.9	30	76.2
¼	6	0.6	10	25.4	31	78.7
½	13	1.3	12	30.5	33	83.8
⅝	16	1.6	13	33.0	34	86.4
¾	19	1.9	14	35.6	35	88.9
⅞	22	2.2	15	38.1	36	91.4
1	25	2.5	16	40.6	37	94.0
1¼	32	3.2	17	43.2	38	96.5
1½	38	3.8	18	45.7	39	99.1
1¾	44	4.4	19	48.3	40	101.6
2	51	5.1	20	50.8	41	104.1
2½	64	6.4	21	53.3	42	106.7
3	76	7.6	22	55.9	43	109.2
3½	89	8.9	23	58.4	44	111.8
4	102	10.2	24	61.0	45	114.3
4½	114	11.4	25	63.5	46	116.8
5	127	12.7	26	66.0	47	119.4
6	152	15.2	27	68.6	48	121.9
7	178	17.8	28	71.1	49	124.5
8	203	20.3	29	73.7	50	127.0

yards to meters

yards	meters	yards	meters	yards	meters	yards	meters	yards	meters
⅛	0.11	2⅛	1.94	4⅛	3.77	6⅛	5.60	8⅛	7.43
¼	0.23	2¼	2.06	4¼	3.89	6¼	5.72	8¼	7.54
⅜	0.34	2⅜	2.17	4⅜	4.00	6⅜	5.83	8⅜	7.66
½	0.46	2½	2.29	4½	4.11	6½	5.94	8½	7.77
⅝	0.57	2⅝	2.40	4⅝	4.23	6⅝	6.06	8⅝	7.89
¾	0.69	2¾	2.51	4¾	4.34	6¾	6.17	8¾	8.00
⅞	0.80	2⅞	2.63	4⅞	4.46	6⅞	6.29	8⅞	8.12
1	0.91	3	2.74	5	4.57	7	6.40	9	8.23
1⅛	1.03	3⅛	2.86	5⅛	4.69	7⅛	6.52	9⅛	8.34
1¼	1.14	3¼	2.97	5¼	4.80	7¼	6.63	9¼	8.46
1⅜	1.26	3⅜	3.09	5⅜	4.91	7⅜	6.74	9⅜	8.57
1½	1.37	3½	3.20	5½	5.03	7½	6.86	9½	8.69
1⅝	1.49	3⅝	3.31	5⅝	5.14	7⅝	6.97	9⅝	8.80
1¾	1.60	3¾	3.43	5¾	5.26	7¾	7.09	9¾	8.92
1⅞	1.71	3⅞	3.54	5⅞	5.37	7⅞	7.20	9⅞	9.03
2	1.83	4	3.66	6	5.49	8	7.32	10	9.14

Index